A MA
MINI
TO T

A MANUAL FOR MINISTRY TO THE SICK

Martin Dudley

First published in Great Britain 1997
Society for Promoting Christian Knowledge
Holy Trinity Church
Marylebone Road
London NW1 4DU

British Library Cataloguing-in-Publication Data

A catalogue record of this book is available from
the British Library

ISBN 0-281-04903-3

Typeset by Pioneer Associates, Perthshire
Printed in Great Britain by
The Cromwell Press, Melksham, Wiltshire

You are to care for all alike, young and old, strong and weak, rich and poor, in the name of him who came not to be served to but to serve.

(Welsh Ordinal)

CONTENTS

	Acknowledgements	ix
	Foreword by the Bishop of London	xi
	Key to Prayer Sources	xiii
	Introduction	1
	How to use this book	7
1	Prayers of Preparation	9
2	Visitation of the Sick	14
3	Prayers for the Sick and Anxious	22
4	Communion of the Sick at Home or in Hospital	41
5	Confession and Absolution	58
6	Laying On of Hands and Anointing	62
7	Rites with the Dying	73
8	Further Prayers After Death	82
9	Comforting the Bereaved: Prayers for a Vigil	86
10	Emergency Baptism	89
11	Blessings of Water, Oil, Persons, and Homes	91
12	Readings, Collects and Psalms	98
13	Pastoral Directory: Guidance on Various Aspects of the Rites	111
	Index of Topics	125
	Index of Prayers	
	(a) by subject	126
	(b) by first line	127

ACKNOWLEDGEMENTS

Material from the following sources is acknowledged:

Prayers from *A Prayer Book for Australia* © 1995 The Anglican Church of Australia Trust Corporation, published by Broughton Books.

Prayers from *A New Zealand Prayer Book* © 1989 The Church of the Province of New Zealand.

Prayer by David Silk from *Prayers for Use at the Alternative Services* © 1980 Mowbray, a Cassel imprint.

Prayers from *Ministry to the Sick* © The Central Board of Finance of the Church of England 1983 and *The Promise of His Glory* © The Central Board of Finance of the Church of England 1991.

Prayers from *Occasional Services: A Companion to Lutheran Book of Worship* © 1982.

Prayers from *The Priest's Vade Mecum* © 1945 SPCK.

Prayers from *A Proposed Prayer Book* © 1952 SPCK and from *The Supplement to the Book of Common Prayer* © 1961 ISPCK.

Prayers from *The Book of Occasional Services* © 1979 The Church Pension Fund.

Rights in Britain and the Commonwealth to material from The Book of Common Prayer, 1662, is vested in the Crown; it is reproduced by permission of the Crown's patentee, Cambridge University Press.

FOREWORD

Christians are called to serve Christ in their neighbours.
When we stand by a sick bed or attend the dying, we are
to be there with the respect and the tenderness which is
appropriate to being in the presence of Christ. There
should be no room for any kind of exploitation of a
person's vulnerability at such moments, but rather the
note of gentleness and attention.

The visitor by the bedside of the sick and dying should
be full of invitation and encouragement in a situation
where especially the dying can often be made to feel that
they are in the way and an embarrassment. It is good to
have the resource and inspiration of traditional prayers at
such moments.

Martin Dudley's book, in the tradition of the *Vade
Mecum*, is a helpful resource for those who minister to the
sick and dying. It uses both established and contemporary
material and in so doing celebrates the persistent
freshness of Christian faith and prayer.

I commend this book to you and hope that it may play
its part in channelling God's grace to times of distress
and affliction. John Donne sums up the experience of our
faith at such moments, 'God comes to thee, not as in the
dawning of the day, not as in the bud of Spring, but as
the sun at noon to illustrate all shadows . . . all occasions
invite his mercies and all times are his seasons.'

✠ Richard London

KEY TO PRAYER SOURCES

[1] *The Alternative Service Book 1980*
[2] The Book of Common Prayer for use in the Church in Wales
[3] *Praying with HIV and AIDS*
[4] The Book of Common Prayer (American Episcopal Church, 1979)
[5] *The Promise of His Glory*
[6] *Occasional Services: A Companion to Lutheran Book of Worship*
[7] *A Prayer Book for Australia*
[8] *A New Zealand Prayer Book*
[9] The Book of Common Prayer (1662)
[10] *The Priest's Vade Mecum*
[11] *The Supplement to the Book of Common Prayer* (India, 1960)
[12] Francis McNutt, *The Prayer Manual*
[13] The Book of Common Prayer (Episcopal Church of Scotland, 1929)
[14] *The Cuddesdon Office Book*
[15] John Henry Newman
[16] David Silk, *Prayers for Use at the Alternative Services*
[17] Martin Dudley
[18] *A Proposed Prayer Book* (India, 1952)
[19] *The Book of Occasional Services*, 2nd edn
[20] *Draft Canadian Prayer Book* (1959)

INTRODUCTION

An apocryphal story is told of a residential meeting of
the House of Bishops. During a social time one of the
bishops suddenly and unexpectedly collapsed. The
Archbishop of Canterbury rushed to his side. He
muttered something. 'He wants to be anointed,' said the
Archbishop, turning to his chaplain, 'Get me an ASB.'
'There is no order for anointing in the ASB, Your Grace,'
said the Chaplain. The sick bishop spoke again. 'He
wants me to hear his confession,' said the Archbishop,
'Pass me an ASB.' 'There is no order for confession in the
ASB, Your Grace,' said the Chaplain. The bishop breathed
his last. 'He's dead,' said the Archbishop. 'There *is* a
funeral service,' said the Chaplain.

The omission from the Alternative Service Book of
pastoral rites for the sick and dying has always seemed
extraordinary. It is not just that they are missing for the
minister. They are also missing for the member of the
congregation who flicks through an ASB in some idle
moment before or during a service. There is no provision
for the sick and that reduces or removes entirely the
expectation of such a ministry. The supplementary book
Ministry to the Sick provided some remedies but was
never really suited to parochial ministry or readily
available to the laity. It assumes in all its rites that there
will be other people present. By contrast, clergy and lay
ministers alike are well used to visiting the sick alone,
one to one, in their homes, in residential care or in
hospital.

This small manual is, in a way, a descendant of *The
Priest's Vade Mecum*, prepared by T. W. Crafer for the

Guild of St Raphael and first published by SPCK in 1945. It will also, inevitably, have its limitations. It is too much to expect any book to provide us with resources for every pastoral situation. Nevertheless, I hope that it will meet its primary purpose – that of being a single, manageable volume that can be easily put in a pocket or briefcase and which will provide most of the texts needed when visiting the acutely and chronically sick and the dying. It has grown from my own pastoral and parochial experience as a curate in Whitchurch (Cardiff), as Vicar of Weston and Priest in charge of Ardeley in North Hertfordshire, and as Vicar of Owlsmoor in Berkshire. Our ability to provide pastoral care depends a good deal on those who form us, correct us, support us and encourage us. The dedication of this book repays some of those debts. One requires some further comment. Elizabeth James was the last name on the list of house communions given to me in June 1979 by my first vicar, Bill Winton. Old enough to be my grandmother, she was meticulous about addressing me as 'Father'. Her flat was a place of welcome and refuge after a long morning taking the sacrament to the sick. She became my good friend, gently chiding when necessary, offering praise when deserved, always supportive. Unable to come to church services, she listened eagerly for reports of the curate's sermons. We kept in touch after I moved to Weston. Childless herself, she would occasionally ask if Paula and I were planning a family. In 1988, when she was very ill, I was able to convey the news that Paula was pregnant. The following year, just a little time before she died, she held our son Thomas in her arms. It was as if she was determined to live to see him. During my year at St Michael's College, Llandaff, Norman Autton taught me a great deal about ministry to the sick. No better teacher could be found. Elizabeth James made that ministry a reality for me and made me much better at it. She ministered to me as much as I to her, and her ministry came out of great personal weakness and a deep reliance on God.

This collection, though acknowledging many debts, is deliberately Anglican in ethos. There will be points of intersection with the Pastoral Care of the Sick provided in the Roman ritual but it has not been a major source for this work. The basic reason for this is that the Roman liturgy rests on a coherent theological anthropology, reinforced by canon law, which differs significantly from a broadly Anglican position. At a most basic level this difference concerns the understanding of the sacraments and the means by which sins are forgiven. The English Book of Common Prayer (1662) also had a coherent anthropology which was expressed and worked out in its rites and prayers. The anthropology of *The Alternative Service Book 1980* is unclear, indeed it might be more honest to say that it is confused. Rejecting the Prayer Book understanding of suffering and sickness, it provided no alternative. The 1979 Book of Common Prayer of the American Episcopal Church (and its supplementary books) has a more systematic understanding of human life, and a number of other prayer books of the Anglican Communion have adopted some of the principles from that book. This collection takes its impetus from the American rather than the English liturgy. It begins from a basic idea that it is in God that we live and move and have our being and that we need divine protection as we face the dangers and adversities of life. Sickness is just such an adversity; sometimes but not necessarily or always a consequence of individual sin, yet a symptom of a broken humanity and a creation marred by sinfulness. Divine grace perfects our nature which is not so deformed that it

3

must be destroyed but which nevertheless requires redemption. The Church's pastoral and sacramental care begins before birth and continues until after death.

I have tried to make this manual of use to those of varying church backgrounds, but I have done this by inclusion rather than by exclusion. My own commitment is to the Catholic movement within the Anglican Church and that is reflected to some degree in my choice of texts, notably a number of older Anglo-Catholic prayers and formulae. Some may take exception to certain of the prayers and rites I have included here; there is, of course, no obligation to use them and they should not be taken as, in any sense, an official or semi-official statement of Anglican doctrine or devotion. I have also expected that this Manual will be used by women who have been ordained to the priesthood and have used both 'him' and 'her', 'he' and 'she' when speaking of priests. Some may take exception to this but I have personally come to accept and value the priestly ministry of women and could not, with integrity, exclude them from this book.

Studies of ritual must increasingly be taken into consideration by liturgists but the ritual workshop is to be found in the community of faith and not in the study. I have, therefore, not attempted to create new rituals, though I was attracted by a sixteenth-century healing ritual recorded by the Venetian Inquisition. A female healer, known as la Draga, put olive leaves in the form of a cross on the forehead of those suffering from headaches, told of a conversation between Lazarus and the Blessed Virgin Mary, and invoked God in highly poetic form. We have lost much of the drama of ministry to the sick and though I believe we must learn how to recover it I have not presumed to make any prescription concerning the ways in which this might be done.

It is now my privilege to be Rector of the Priory Church of St Bartholomew the Great, neighbour to the renowned and threatened hospital that also bears the Apostle's name. Rahere, who founded both hospital and priory in 1123 and whose mortal remains are still in his tomb in the sanctuary, did so as a result of an intense and life-threatening experience of both sickness and sin. One cannot minister here without being well aware of the close relation between physical and spiritual well-being and the need to provide healing for bodies and souls. I hope this book will be an aid to this ministry.

I would like to acknowledge the help given me by my wife Paula, Senior Lecturer in the Division of Podiatric Medicine at the University of Westminster, for providing a broader perspective on health and sickness informed by her professional concerns in medical anthropology. My thanks are also due to my new bishop, Richard Chartres, for writing the Foreword, to the Revd Peter Cowell, Chaplain of the Royal London Hospital, for advice on relations with hospital chaplains, to Bishop George Hacker, and the Revd Michael Burden of the Guild of St Raphael, and to the Revd Jim Woodward for many stimulating conversations on the subjects central to this manual. Finally, I am enormously grateful to Rachel Boulding at SPCK who has ensured that this book reached completion and advocated a number of wise additions and improvements.

HOW TO USE THIS BOOK

This book consists of a collection of rites, prayers and readings suitable for a wide variety of pastoral situations, ranging from emergency baptism to the blessing of a house, but with a strong focus on ministry to the sick and the dying. The texts are drawn from many sources, traditional and modern, including authorized texts from a number of Anglican provinces. I have generally assumed that only the minister has a printed text and so have not included responses and litanies other than with the most simple responses. I strongly recommend a careful preliminary reading of all the material. The sign ✠ is used in the text at points where it would be appropriate for a priest to make the sign of the cross toward a person to whom he or she is ministering.

In the hope of increasing the usefulness of this manual, there are both traditional and modern language prayers included in most sections. By careful choice it is possible to stay with one form of language for most forms of ministry. There are three versions of the Communion of the Sick: Prayer Book, Rite B and Rite A. Some of the readings are from the Authorized Version and some from the New Revised Standard Version. Some of the psalms are from the Prayer Book Psalter and some from the American Book of Common Prayer 1979 (the psalter used in *Celebrating Common Prayer*). A book of prayers is a useful prompt, but when faced by times of crisis or sorrow, of joy and thanksgiving, the minister should always be prepared to give voice to what is felt in his or her own words. Some of the prayers here, inadequate or not specific enough for your purposes, may provide a frame for your own expressions. A key to the sources of the prayers here can be found on page xiii.

At the back of the book is a Pastoral Directory. It is a concise guide to good practice. It covers basic material about the use of the rites but also offers important reminders about behaviour, confidentiality and working with other professionals. It should be read before any of the rites are used. For some, it will be no more than a clarification of things already known; for others, it may be an indication of better ways of doing things.

The term 'Minister' here refers to any person authorized to perform this ministry – lay or ordained. Within the Anglican tradition, certain types of blessing and absolution are reserved to bishops and priests.

Prayers and rites have been written using male and female interchangeably in the singular, and should be adapted as appropriate for the opposite gender or for groups.

1 PRAYERS OF PREPARATION

Those who minister to the sick need to be prepared. In a busy pastoral ministry we rush constantly from one thing to another. Stop for a moment at least, even if it is only in the car before a visit to a sick person at home or in hospital, and pray.

These prayers are suggestions of what might be useful. Above all we should acknowledge our own weakness and inadequacy and ask God to minister through our weakness.

Reflect for a moment on the Ordinal. Its words are relevant to all who minister.

You are to care for all alike, young and old, strong and weak, rich and poor, in the name of him who came not to be served but to serve.   [2]

Because you cannot bear the weight of this ministry in your own strength but only by the grace and power of God, pray earnestly for his Holy Spirit.   [1]

Keep the Good Shepherd always before you as the pattern of your calling.   [2]

Give yourselves wholly to God's service and devote to him your best powers of mind and spirit, so that as you daily follow the rule and teaching of our Lord, with the heavenly assistance of his Holy Spirit, you may grow up into his likeness, and sanctify the lives of all with whom you have to do.   [1]

Recall, as well, the words of Scripture.

You did not choose me but I chose you. And I appointed
you to go and bear fruit, fruit that will last, so that the
Father will give you whatever you ask him in my name.

(John 15.16 RSV)

Lord Jesus, I do not find it easy to minister to those who
    are sick.
They make me so aware of my own weakness and
    inadequacy.
They bring so many of my fears to the fore.
I seem so inadequate to meet their needs.
In my weakness may I find strength in you.
Teach me to be silent and still, a sign of your presence.
May my hands minister your healing
and my words bring your comfort and consolation.
Let me be the means and instrument of your ministry.

[17]

O Lord Jesus Christ, God's Word of Love,
converting, consoling, healing and comforting,
enlivening, empowering, liberating and redeeming,
accept my prayer.
Give me grace and courage to serve you
in the sick and the sorrowing;
By your power enable me fulfil the ministry
to which you have called me
and in all things to give you the glory.   [17]

Jesus, betrayed, hear my prayer.
Jesus, abandoned, hear my prayer.
Jesus, slapped, hear my prayer.
Jesus, whipped, hear my prayer.
Jesus, spat upon, hear my prayer.
Jesus, mocked, hear my prayer.

Jesus, denied, hear my prayer.
Jesus, condemned, hear my prayer.
Jesus, stripped, hear my prayer.
Jesus, crucified, hear my prayer.
Jesus, dying, hear my prayer.
Jesus, buried, hear my prayer.
Jesus, raised, hear my prayer.
Jesus, ascended, hear my prayer.
Jesus, crowned, hear my prayer.
Jesus, known in the breaking of bread, hear my prayer.

[3]

AN INVOCATION OF THE SPIRIT

Holy Spirit, come and be with us,
guide and inspire us,
let us know your power.
Power to heal,
power to comfort,
power to console.
Holy Spirit, come and be with us.   [17]

Familiar prayers are frequently the means by which we may recollect our dependence on God in and for our ministry.

God be in my head:
   and in mine understanding.
God be in mine eyes:
   and in my looking.
God be in my mouth:
   and in my speaking.
God be in my heart:
   and in my thinking.
God be at mine end:
   and at my departing.   [Traditional]

A PRAYER OF ST RICHARD OF CHICHESTER

Thanks be to thee, my Lord Jesus Christ,
for all the benefits which thou hast given me,
for all the pains and insults which thou hast borne
    for me.
O most merciful Redeemer, Friend, and Brother,
may I know thee more clearly
     love thee more dearly,
      follow thee more nearly.   **Amen.**

A PRAYER OF ST IGNATIUS LOYOLA

Teach us, good Lord, to serve thee as thou deservest:
to give and not to count the cost;
to fight and not to heed the wounds;
to toil and not to seek for rest;
to labour and not to ask for any reward,
save that of knowing that we do thy will;
through Jesus Christ our Lord. **Amen.**

ST PATRICK'S BREASTPLATE

Christ be with me, Christ within me,
Christ behind me, Christ before me,
Christ beside me, Christ to win me,
Christ to comfort and restore me,
Christ beneath me, Christ above me,
Christ in quiet, Christ in danger,
Christ in hearts of all that love me,
Christ in mouth of friend and stranger.

I bind unto myself the name
the strong name of the Trinity;
by invocation of the same,
the Three in One and One in Three.
of whom all nature hath creation;
Eternal Father, Spirit, Word:
praise to the Lord of my salvation,
salvation is of Christ the Lord. **Amen.**

Remember, O Lord, what thou hast wrought in us, and
not what we deserve; and as thou hast called us to thy
service, make us worthy of our calling; through Jesus
Christ our Lord. **Amen.** [4]

O Lord God,
whose mercies are sure and full and ever new:
grant us the greatest of them all,
the Spirit of your dear Son;
that in the day of judgement
we may be presented to you
if not blameless, yet forgiven,
if not successful, yet faithful,
if not holy, yet persevering,
deserving nothing, but accepted in him
who pleads our cause and redeemed our lives,
even Jesus Christ our Lord. **Amen.** [5]

2 VISITATION OF THE SICK

No set form provided in a prayer book can ever hope to meet the needs of those who minister to the sick. The 1662 order was never satisfactory. Some would argue that its revisions in the English and American books of 1928 were even worse. This section, together with other sections containing prayers, psalms and readings, sets out to provide resources for visiting the sick in a formal pastoral way. In the manner of a number of contemporary liturgical manuals, it also provides frameworks that can be filled in using material from elsewhere in the book.

OPENING GREETING

On entering the house where a sick person lives, the minister may say

Peace be to this house, and to all that dwell in it.

BIBLICAL SENTENCES

My presence shall go with thee, says the Lord, and I will give thee rest.   (Exodus 33.14)

Only be strong and of good courage.   (Joshua 1.18)

I believe that I shall see the goodness of the Lord in the land of the living. Wait for the Lord; be strong, and let your heart take courage; wait for the Lord!   (Psalm 27.14)

Praise the Lord with me: let us exalt his name together, for I sought the Lord's help and he answered and freed me from all my tears. (Psalm 34.3–4)

For God alone my soul in silence waits; from him comes my salvation. (Psalm 62.1)

My flesh and my heart may fail, but God is the strength of my heart and my portion forever. (Psalm 73.26)

You are my refuge and my stronghold, my God in whom I put my trust. (Psalm 91.2)

Trust in the Lord forever, for in the Lord God you have an everlasting rock. (Isaiah 26.4)

They that wait upon the Lord shall renew their strength.
(Isaiah 40.31)

Heal me, O Lord, and I shall be healed; save me, and I shall be saved; for thou art my praise. (Jeremiah 17.14)

They asked only to touch the hem of Jesus' garment, and all who touched him were healed. (Mark 6.56)

When the sun was setting, all those who had any that were sick with various diseases brought them to Jesus; and he laid his hands on every one of them and healed them. (Luke 4.40)

Let not your heart be troubled: ye believe in God, believe also in me. (John 14.1)

In nothing be anxious: but in everything, by prayer and supplication with thanksgiving, let your requests be made known unto God. And the peace of God, which passeth all understanding, shall keep your hearts and minds in Christ Jesus. (Philippians 4.6, 7)

Fear not; I am the first and the last and the living one; and I was dead, and behold, I am alive for evermore.
(Revelation 1.17–18)

THE COMFORTABLE WORDS

Hear what comfortable words our Saviour Christ saith unto all that truly turn to him:

Come unto me all that travail and are heavy laden, and I will refresh you. (Matthew 11.28)

So God loved the world, that he gave his only-begotten Son, to the end that all that believe in him should not perish, but have everlasting life. (John 3.16)

Hear also what Saint Paul saith:

This is a true saying, and worthy of all men to be received, That Christ Jesus came into the world to save sinners. (1 Timothy 1.15)

Hear also what Saint John saith:

If any man sin, we have an Advocate with the Father, Jesus Christ the righteous; and he is the propitiation for our sins. (1 John 2.1)   [9]

A psalm may be said (see section 16).

Prayers may be said (see section 2).

PROFESSION OF FAITH

The minister may remind the sick person of the importance of faith in God and invite him or her to make a reaffirmation.

Minister Let us affirm our faith in the redeeming love of God, and say

I believe in God the Father Almighty, maker
  of heaven and earth:
and in Jesus Christ, his only Son our Lord,
who was conceived by the Holy Ghost,
born of the Virgin Mary,
suffered under Pontius Pilate,
was crucified, dead and buried:
he descended into hell;
the third day he rose again from the dead;
he ascended into heaven,
and sitteth on the right hand of God the
  Father Almighty;
from thence he shall come to judge the quick
  and the dead.
I believe in the Holy Ghost; the holy
  Catholic Church;
the communion of saints; the forgiveness
  of sins;
the resurrection of the body; and the life
  everlasting. **Amen.**

or

Minister I invite you to renew your profession of the Christian faith into which you were baptized.

17

Minister	Do you believe and trust in God the Father, who made the world?
Reply	**I believe and trust in him.**
Minister	Do you believe and trust in his Son Jesus Christ, who redeemed mankind?
Reply	**I believe and trust in him.**
Minister	Do you believe and trust in his Holy Spirit, who gives life to the people of God?
Reply	**I believe and trust in him.**
Minister	This is the faith of the Church.
Reply	**We believe and trust in one God, Father, Son and Holy Spirit.** [1]

REPENTANCE

Provision is made in section 6 for sacramental confession and absolution; nevertheless, some more familiar form may appropriately be used by those not used to auricular confession.

The minister encourages the sick person to examine his or her conscience. The sick person should be reminded of the need to forgive all by whom he or she has been offended, to seek forgiveness for offence given, and to resolve to make amends. Confession may be made using any familiar form. In times of need, the minister may say the confession in the name of the sick person who, at the end, says Amen.

All	**Almighty God, Father of our Lord Jesus Christ, Maker of all things, Judge of all**

men: we acknowledge and bewail our manifold sins and wickedness, which we, from time to time, most grievously have committed, by thought, word, and deed, against thy divine majesty, provoking most justly thy wrath and indignation against us. We do earnestly repent, and are heartily sorry for these our misdoings; the remembrance of them is grievous unto us; the burden of them is intolerable. Have mercy upon us, have mercy upon us, most merciful Father; for thy Son our Lord Jesus Christ's sake, forgive us all that is past; and grant that we may ever hereafter serve and please thee in newness of life, to the honour and glory of thy name; through Jesus Christ our Lord. Amen.

Minister   Almighty God, our heavenly Father, who of his great mercy hath promised forgiveness of sins to all them that with hearty repentance and true faith turn unto him: have mercy ✠ upon *you*; pardon and deliver *you* from all *your* sins; confirm and strengthen *you* in all goodness; and bring *you* to everlasting life; through Jesus Christ our Lord. **Amen.**   [9]

or

All   **Almighty God, our heavenly Father,**
           we have sinned against thee,
           through our own fault,
           in thought, and word and deed,
           and in what we have left undone.

19

We are heartily sorry
and repent of all our sins.
For thy Son our Lord Jesus Christ's sake,
forgive us all that is past;
and grant that we may serve thee
   in newness of life,
to the glory of thy name.   **Amen.**

Minister   Almighty God,
who forgives all who truly repent,
have mercy upon *you*, ✠
pardon and deliver *you* from all your sins,
confirm and strengthen *you* in all goodness,
and keep *you* in life eternal;
through Jesus Christ our Lord. **Amen.**   [1]

or

All   **Almighty God, our heavenly Father,**
we have sinned against you and against our
   neighbours,
in thought, and word, and deed,
through negligence, through weakness,
through our own deliberate fault.
We are truly sorry
and repent of all our sins.
For the sake of your Son Jesus Christ,
   who died for us,
forgive us all that is past;
and grant that we may serve you in newness
   of life,
to the glory of your name.   Amen.   [1]

Minister   Almighty God,
who forgives all who truly repent,
have mercy upon *you*, ✠
pardon and deliver *you* from all *your* sins,
confirm and strengthen *you* in all goodness,
and keep *you* in life eternal;
through Jesus Christ our Lord. **Amen.**

LAYING ON OF HANDS, ANOINTING AND COMMUNION

The visitation may include any or all of these rites
(see sections 5 and 7).

3 PRAYERS FOR THE SICK AND ANXIOUS

Spoken prayers can be extremely helpful but we do not need to fill every space with them. Just being there is important. Silence can be upholding.

A GENERAL INTERCESSION

Minister   Let us beseech the Lord, mighty and pitiful, for all who in this transitory life are in trouble, sorrow, need, sickness, or any other adversity:

for the bereaved and sorrowful;
for widows and orphans;
for the lonely and unloved.

All   **We beseech thee, O Lord.**

For women in labour;
for suffering children;
for the naked and hungry;

All   **We beseech thee, O Lord.**

For those who face danger;
for those who travel by land or sea or in the air;
for the anxious and uncertain;

All   **We beseech thee, O Lord.**

For the aged and weak;
for the disabled and handicapped;
for the blind, the deaf, and those unable
   to speak;

All   **We beseech thee, O Lord.**

For the sleepless and fevered;
for the injured and wounded;
for those in great pain;

All   **We beseech thee, O Lord.**

For those weary with suffering;
for the bedridden and housebound;
for those sick unto death;

All   **We beseech thee, O Lord.**

For the ministries of healing;
for doctors and nurses;
for pastors and priests;

All   **We beseech thee, O Lord.**

*This litany may be concluded with a prayer drawn from
this section.*

FOR THE SICK AND DYING

O gracious Lord Jesus, who didst vouchsafe to die upon
   the cross for us,

23

remember, we beseech thee, all sick and dying persons,
and grant that they may omit nothing which is necessary
   to make their peace with thee before they die.
Deliver them, O Lord, from the malice of the devil, and
   from all sin and evil,
and grant them a happy end, for thy loving mercy's sake.
Amen.

FOR ANY SICK PERSON

O God, who alone canst strengthen the weakness of
man, show forth thy mighty help unto this thy sick
servant, that by thy merciful aid *he* may be restored
whole to thy Church; through Jesus Christ our Lord.
Amen.   [10]

FOR ALL WHO SUFFER

O Lord of all grace and blessing, behold, visit and relieve
   thy sick servants.
Look upon them with the eyes of thy mercy,
give them comfort and sure confidence in thee,
defend them from the danger of the enemy,
and keep them in perpetual peace;
through Christ our Lord.   **Amen.**   [9 altered]

Hear us, Almighty and most merciful God and Saviour;
extend thy accustomed goodness to thy servants who are
   grieved with sickness.   **Amen.**

Sanctify this trial unto them, that the sense of their
weakness may add strength to their faith, and
seriousness to their repentance.   **Amen.**

24

May it be thy good pleasure to restore them to their former health, that so they may live the rest of their lives in thy fear and to thy glory. **Amen.**

And whatsoever the issue that thou shalt ordain for them, give them grace to be so conformed to thy will, that they may be made meet to dwell with thee in life everlasting; through Jesus Christ our Lord. **Amen.** [11]

Merciful Lord, you sent your Son to be our peace.
Help all who suffer pain or grief to find in him strength
    and peace,
so that their trust in your promises may be renewed;
through Jesus Christ our Lord. **Amen.** [6]

FOR ALL WHO DESIRE PRAYERS

Blessed Lord, we ask your loving care and protection for
    those who are sick in body, mind, or spirit and who
    desire our prayers.
Take from them all fears and help them to put their
    trust in you,
that they may feel your strong arms around them.
Touch them with your renewing love,
that they may know wholeness in you and glorify
    your name;
through Jesus Christ our Lord. **Amen.** [6]

FOR HEALING

O God, who by the prayers of thy holy Apostles didst restore the sick to life, grant, we pray thee, that by the ministrations of thy holy Church, this thy servant may be restored to spiritual health, and if it be thy will also to bodily health; through Jesus Christ our Lord. **Amen.**

O Lord Jesus Christ, who by the power of thy word didst heal all who were brought unto thee in the days of thy flesh, mercifully help thy servant in *his* hour of need: grant, if it be thy will, that by the same power *he* may be delivered from sickness and restored to health, and may for ever hereafter serve thee in newness of life to the glory of thy name; who livest and reignest with the Father and the Holy Ghost, ever one God, world without end. **Amen.** [10]

O almighty Father, who dost heal both the bodies and souls of men, who didst send thine only-begotten Son, our Lord Jesus Christ, to heal every sickness and disease, and to redeem us from death, deliver this thy servant, we humbly beseech thee, from all infirmities, both of body and soul, which do hinder *him*, and quicken *him* by the grace of thy Christ; for thou art the fountain of healing, O our God, and unto thee do we give the glory with thine only-begotten Son, who with thee and the Holy Ghost liveth and reigneth ever one God, world without end. **Amen.** [10]

O holy Lord, almighty Father, everlasting God, who dost confirm the frailty of our nature by pouring upon it thine exceeding goodness, that our limbs and bodies may be strengthened by the healthful medicine of thy mercy: look graciously upon this thy servant, that *he* may be freed from the hands of all bodily infirmity, and by thy merciful favour *his* former health may be renewed; through Jesus Christ our Lord. **Amen.** [10]

Sovereign Lord, our God, Almighty, we beseech thee
    save us all,
thou only Physician of souls and bodies.

Sanctify us all, thou that healest every disease; and heal
    especially this thy servant.
raise *him* up from the bed of pain by thy tender
    loving-kindness;
visit *him* in mercy and compassion;
drive away from *him* all sickness and infirmity;
that, being raised up by thy mighty hand, *he* may serve
    thee with all thankfulness;
and that we, being made partakers of thy goodness,
may praise and glorify thee,
who doest works great and wonderful and worthy to be
    praised.
For it is thine to pity and to save; and to thee we ascribe
    glory,
Father, Son, and Holy Spirit, now and for evermore.

Amen.   [10]

God of grace and comfort enfold *N* with your mercy.
Strengthen *her* with the shield of faith,
and enable *her* to accept what is to come;
heal *her* and bear *her* pain,
keep *her* in peace, and fix *her* heart on you;
through Jesus Christ our Lord.   **Amen.**   [7]

Lord Jesus Christ,
Son of the living and life-giving God,
you vanquished the powers of evil
and healed those who were sick;
send your Holy Spirit on our *sister N*,
restore *her* to health
and confirm *her* trust in you,
through your all-powerful name.   **Amen.**   [7]

O Lord, who always hears our prayers,
give *N* your gift of healing
for we cannot bear to see *him* suffer;
and if it cannot be that he should be healed,
take him to yourself, we pray,
so that *he* knows no more pain or tears. **Amen.**   [17]

FOR THE HEALING OF MEMORIES

Loving God, merciful and forgiving,
in your hands are all times and ages,
our past, present and future.
Grant an experience of your generous love to those who
    suffer from past hurts.
Heal their memories, cleanse their minds,
renew their hope and confidence,
and make them whole.
We ask this through Christ our Lord. **Amen.**

FOR RECONCILIATION BETWEEN PERSONS

God of peace, forgive us all as we forgive each other for
    all the hurt we have brought into our lives.
Let your healing love rest upon the wounds we have
    caused by our anger.
Deepen our love in a new understanding of each other
    and for you.
We ask this in the name of Jesus Christ
who carried on his cross our discord and our grief.

Amen.

FOR RECOVERY FROM SICKNESS

O God the strength of the weak and the comfort of
sufferers, mercifully accept our prayers and grant to your
servant N, the help of your power, that *his* sickness may
be turned into health and our sorrow into joy; through
Jesus Christ our Lord. **Amen.** [4]

O God of heavenly powers,
by the might of your command you drive away from our
    bodies all sickness and all infirmity:
Be present in your goodness with your servant N,
that *her* weakness may be banished and *her* strength
    restored;
and that *her* health being renewed *she* may bless your
    holy name;
through Jesus Christ our Lord. **Amen.** [4]

We rejoice, Lord, that N is well again;
we thank you for your gift of healing
and pray that *he* may continue in strength
and be maintained in your love
all the days of *his* life. **Amen.** [17]

FOR A SICK CHILD

Lord Jesus Christ, Good Shepherd of the sheep,
you gather the lambs in your arms and carry them in
    your bosom.
We commend to your loving care this child N.
Relieve *her* pain, guard *her* from all danger,
restore to *her* your gifts of gladness and strength,
and raise *her* up to a life of service to you.
Hear us, we pray, for your dear name's sake. **Amen.** [4]

29

Heavenly Father, watch with us over your child *N*,
and grant that *he* may be restored to that perfect health
    which it is yours alone to give,
through Jesus Christ our Lord. **Amen.**   [4]

FOR THOSE WHO MINISTER TO THE SICK

Grant, O merciful God, we pray,
for all who minister healing and comfort to the sick and
    suffering,
your protection when they perform their duty,
strength and patience, tenderness and love for all,
that they may faithfully serve you in their service of
    others. **Amen.**   [12]

Almighty God, source of human knowledge and skill,
guide physicians and nurses and all those you have
called to practice the arts of healing. Strengthen them by
your life-giving Spirit, that, by their ministries, the health
of all people may be promoted and your creation
glorified; through Jesus Christ our Lord. **Amen.**   [6]

O Lord of the day and of the night, be with your
    servants as they watch over *N*.
Give them strength when they are tired,
patience when restless,
encouragement when down-hearted. **Amen.**   [17]

FOR A PERSON RECEIVING MINISTRY AND
THOSE MINISTERING

Almighty God, giver of life and health,
hear our prayers for *N*,
that by your blessing on *her* and on those who minister
    to *her*,

she may be restored to health of body and mind
according to your will,
and in the presence of your people give thanks to you;
through Jesus Christ our Lord. **Amen.**   [7]

FOR A BLESSING ON SUFFERING

With painful footsteps, O blessed Lord, you carried the
cross to Calvary;
help us to take up our cross and so to follow you.
As we walk where you have walked and tread where
you have trod,
may our suffering make us like you,
and so may we come at last to your kingdom and see
you in glory,
where you live and reign with the Father and the
Holy Spirit,
one God, for ever and ever. **Amen.**   [17, based on 10]

FOR THOSE IN GREAT PAIN

O gracious Father, whose dear Son bore for us
unspeakable agonies,
being scourged, and crowned with thorns, and nailed to
the cross:
have mercy on thy servant who is now in great suffering,
and grant *him* grace to fix *his* eyes upon the cross,
and to find strength there to copy the example of him
who,
for the joy that was set before him, endured the cross;
that following *his* Divine Master through suffering,
he may follow him to his eternal glory;
through the same thy Son Jesus Christ our Lord.
Amen.   [10]

FOR THOSE WHO SUFFER
(A PRAYER OF THE FIRST WORLD WAR, FRANCE 1915)

O Lord God, our heavenly Father, regard, we beseech
thee, with thy divine pity the pains of all thy children;
and grant that the Passion of the Lord and his infinite
love may make fruitful for good the tribulations of the
innocent, the sufferings of the sick, and the sorrows of
the bereaved; through him who suffered in our flesh and
died for our sake, the same thy Son our Saviour Jesus
Christ. **Amen.**   [13]

INVOKING THE PASSION OF CHRIST

O Lord Jesu Christ, Son of the living God,
we pray thee to set thy passion, cross, and death
between thy judgement and our souls,
now and in the hour of our death.
Vouchsafe to grant mercy and grace to the living, rest to
    the dead,
to thy holy Church peace and concord,
and to us sinners everlasting life and glory;
who with the Father and the Holy Spirit livest and
    reignest,
world without end.   **Amen.**   [4]

FOR THOSE WHO WATCH WITH THE SICK OR
DYING – CHRIST'S WATCH IN THE GARDEN

God of the dark night,
you were with Jesus praying in the garden,
you were with Jesus all the way to the cross
and through to the resurrection.

Help us to recognize you now, as we watch with *N*
and wait for what must happen;
help us through any bitterness and despair,
help us to accept our distress,
help us to remember that you care for us
and that in your will is our peace. **Amen.**   [8]

FOR THOSE IN SEVERE PAIN – THE SUFFERING OF CHRIST

Jesus, you knew pain,
you knew the loneliness, the weakness
and the degradation it brings;
you knew the agony.
Jesus, your suffering is the only hope,
the only reconciliation for those who suffer.
Be with *N* as *she* grapples with the pain *she* suffers now.
Be a promise to *her*
that this present suffering will cease;
be the hand that *she* can hold;
be present Saviour, for we need you now. **Amen.**   [8]

FOR THE MINISTRY OF FAMILY AND FRIENDS

Loving God, our creator and redeemer,
give strength and gentleness, patience and faithfulness
to family members and friends.
Let their hope be in you
and by their ministry of love let your love be known;
through Jesus Christ our Lord. **Amen.**   [6]

BEFORE AN OPERATION

Almighty God, our heavenly Father, we beseech thee
graciously to comfort thy servant in *his* suffering, and to
bless the means made use of for *his* cure. Fill his heart
with confidence, that though *he* be sometime afraid, *he*
yet may put his trust in thee; through Jesus Christ our
Lord. **Amen.**   [4]

God of compassion and mercy,
you never fail to help and comfort those who seek
    your aid;
give strength and peace to this your servant,
and enable *her* to know that you are near.
Give wisdom and care to those who minister to *her*
(especially . . .),
grant that *she* may have no fear since you are with *her*.
                                        Amen.   [7]

PRAYERS BEFORE CHILDBIRTH

O blessed Jesus, to bring us salvation
you did not abhor the Virgin's womb.
In the fullness of time you were born of a woman
and shared our human life and death.
Be present with your servant soon to give birth.
May she trust in you, the source of all life.
Give her strength and patience,
protect her against all the dangers and pains of labour,
    so that she may be safely delivered
and turn to you with joy and thanksgiving.
We ask this for your tender mercy's sake. **Amen.**   [17]

34

O God, the creator and sustainer of life,
graciously preserve and protect N during childbirth
and safely bring forth in health and wholeness
the infant whom you have created;
through Jesus Christ our Lord. **Amen.** [6]

O Lord our God, creator of all that exists, we thank you
for the joy of watching new life begin and for the privilege
of sharing with you in your continuing creation. In your
mercy grant that these blessings may continue to us and
even to our children's children, that generations yet
unborn may bless your holy name; through Jesus Christ
our Lord. **Amen.** [6]

FOR THOSE MAKING DECISIONS

In the American Lutheran book, Occasional Services, *this
prayer is described as appropriate for those who are deciding
which treatment to follow in an illness or affliction, how long
to continue life-support systems, or where to spend days of
recovery or growing older.*

O Lord our God, send your Holy Spirit to guide us,
that we may make our decisions with love, mercy,
and reverence for your gift of life;
through Jesus Christ our Lord. **Amen.** [6]

FOR THOSE WHO ARE CRITICALLY ILL OR FACING GREAT UNCERTAINTY

God of the present moment,
God who in Jesus stills the storm
and soothes the frantic heart;
bring hope and courage to N

as *he* waits in uncertainty.
Bring hope that you will make *him* the equal of whatever
  lies ahead.
Bring *him* courage to endure what cannot be avoided,
for your will is health and wholeness;
you are our God and we need you.   **Amen.**   [8]

FOR THE AGED

O Lord God, look with mercy on all for whom increasing
tears bring isolation and distress. Give them
understanding helpers and the willingness to accept
help; and as their strength diminishes, increase their
faith and their assurance of your love. We pray in the
name of Jesus Christ our Lord.   **Amen.**   [4]

Eternal God, whose years extend through all
generations, we have but a short span of life and we
wear out as a garment. May old age bring us wisdom,
contentment and a deep longing to be with thee for all
eternity.   **Amen.**   [7 adapted]

God of the unknown,
as age draws in on us, irresistible as the tide,
make our life's last quarter the best that there has been.
As our strength ebbs, release our inner vitality,
all you have taught us over the years;
as our energy diminishes
increase our compassion, and educate our prayer.
You have made us human to share your divine life;
grant us the first-fruits.   **Amen.**   [8]

IN LIFE-THREATENING ILLNESS

God, our refuge,
when human resources fail,
you alone remain our sure hope and defence.
Grant us courage as we place ourselves
    (and *N*) in your hands,
confident that nothing can separate us from your love.
                                        Amen.   [7 adapted]

IN DOUBT AND WHEN FAITH
IS UNDER TEST

Almighty God, our heavenly Father,
what you ask us to bear at times we find hard to
    understand.
Sometimes we feel angry and confused,
when your care and purpose seem distant,
and we fear that in our faith we have been deceived.
Yet we believe that you are still our heavenly Father,
and we long to know that your love has not lost control.
Strengthen our faith and assure us of your gracious
    compassion;
through Jesus Christ our Lord. **Amen.**   [7]

THANKSGIVING FOR HEALING

Merciful Lord God, constant source of healing, we give
you thanks for all your gifts of strength and life, and
above all we thank you for the gift of your Son, through
whom we have health and salvation. As we wait for that
day when there will be no more pain, help us by your
Holy Spirit to be assured of your power in our lives and
to trust in your eternal love; through Jesus Christ our
Lord. **Amen.**   [6]

God of steadfast love,
your mercies are new every day:
we thank you for healing *N*.
We give you thanks for the love of *her* family and friends,
for the prayers of your people,
and for those who have ministered your healing
through the power of Jesus Christ. **Amen.**   [7 adapted]

AT THE END OF AN EVENING VISIT

Be our light in the darkness, O Lord,
and in your great mercy defend us from all perils and
    dangers of this night;
for the love of your only Son, our Saviour Jesus Christ.
                                        Amen.   [9]

Be present, O merciful God,
and protect us through the silent hours of this night,
so that we who are wearied by the changes and chances
    of this life
may rest in your eternal changelessness;
through Jesus Christ our Lord. **Amen.**   [4]

Look down, O Lord, from your heavenly throne,
and illumine this night with your celestial brightness,
that by night as by day your people may glorify your
    holy name;
through Jesus Christ our Lord. **Amen.**   [4]

Visit this place, O Lord,
and drive far from it all snares of the enemy;
let your holy angels dwell with us to preserve us in
    peace,
and let your blessing be upon us always;
through Jesus Christ our Lord. **Amen.**   [4]

AT THE END OF THE DAY

Keep watch, dear Lord, with those who work or watch
   or weep this night,
and give your angels charge over those who sleep.
Tend the sick, Lord Christ; give rest to the weary, bless
   the dying,
soothe the suffering, pity the afflicted, shield the joyous;
and all for your love's sake. **Amen.** [4]

Into thy hands, O Father and Lord,
we commend this night our souls and bodies,
our homes and families, neighbours and kindred,
our benefactors and brethren departed,
all folk rightly believing,
and all who need thy pity and protection.
Light us with thy holy grace,
and suffer us never to be separated from thee,
O Lord in Trinity, God everlasting. **Amen.** [14]

ANIMA CHRISTI

Soul of Christ, sanctify me;
Body of Christ, save me;
Blood of Christ, refresh me;
Water from the side of Christ, wash me;
Passion of Christ, strengthen me;
O good Jesu, hear me;
within thy wounds hide me;
suffer me not to be separated from thee;
from the malicious enemy defend me;
in the hour of my death call me;
and bid me come to thee;
that with thy saints I may praise thee;
     through the ages of eternity. **Amen.**

BEFORE THE CRUCIFIX

Lord, by this sweet and saving sign,
defend us from our foes and thine.
> Jesu, by thy wounded feet,
>> direct our path aright.
> Jesu, by thy nailed hands,
>> move ours to deeds of love.
> Jesu, by thy crown of thorns,
>> annihilate our pride.
> Jesu, by thy silence,
>> shame our complaints.
> Jesu, by thy parched lips,
>> curb our cruel speech.
> Jesu, by thy closing eyes,
>> look on our sin no more.
> Jesu, by thy broken heart,
>> knit ours to thee.

And by this sweet and saving sign,
Lord, draw us to our peace and thine. **Amen.**   [14]

4 COMMUNION OF THE SICK AT HOME OR IN HOSPITAL

These rites are for occasions when the sacrament, already consecrated, is brought to the sick person by a priest or lay minister. Three rites are provided. Rite 1 is based on the 1662 Holy Communion and uses the Prayer Book confession. Rite 2 is also in traditional language but follows Rite B in the Alternative Service Book. Rite 3 is in modern language and follows Rite A in the Alternative Service Book.

In these rites for the communion of the sick, the minister will need to make certain adaptations, according to circumstances. The rites have been written in the singular, i.e. for one communicant, alternating male and female, and must be adapted for more than one person receiving communion or for communicants of the opposite sex. Lay ministers should change 'you' to 'us' in the absolution and blessing.

Please read the notes in the Pastoral Directory before using these rites.

Rite 1

Minister   In the name of the Father, and of the Son,
             and of the Holy Ghost. **Amen.**

All   **Almighty God,**
             unto whom all hearts be open,
             all desires known,
             and from whom no secrets are hid:

cleanse the thoughts of our hearts
by the inspiration of the Holy Spirit,
that we may perfectly love thee,
and worthily magnify thy holy name;
through Christ our Lord. Amen

The minister says the collect. One or more readings may be used, normally including a gospel reading. Intercessions may be made.

Minister   Ye that do truly and earnestly repent you of
your sins, and are in love and charity with
your neighbours, and intend to lead a new
life, following the commandments of God,
and walking from henceforth in his holy
ways; draw near with faith, and take this
Holy Sacrament to your comfort; and make
your humble confession to Almighty God,
(meekly kneeling upon your knees).

All   **Almighty God, Father of our Lord Jesus
Christ, Maker of all things, Judge of all
men; we acknowledge and bewail our
manifold sins and wickedness, which we,
from time to time, most grievously have
committed, by thought, word, and deed,
against thy divine majesty, provoking most
justly thy wrath and indignation against us.
We do earnestly repent, and are heartily
sorry for these our misdoings; the
remembrance of them is grievous unto us;
the burden of them is intolerable. Have
mercy upon us, have mercy upon us, most
merciful Father; for thy Son our Lord Jesus
Christ's sake, forgive us all that is past;**

and grant that we may ever hereafter serve
and please thee in newness of life, to the
honour and glory of thy name; through
Jesus Christ our Lord.   Amen.

Minister   Almighty God, our heavenly Father, who of
his great mercy hath promised forgiveness of
sins to all them that with hearty repentance
and true faith turn unto him; have mercy ✠
upon *you*; pardon and deliver *you* from all
your sins; confirm and strengthen *you* in all
goodness; and bring *you* to everlasting life;
through Jesus Christ our Lord.

All   **Amen.**

The Comfortable Words may be said.

Minister   Hear what comfortable words our Saviour
Christ saith unto all that truly turn to him.

Come unto me all that travail and are heavy
laden, and I will refresh you. (Matthew 11.28)

So God loved the world, that he gave his
only-begotten Son, to the end that all that
believe in him should not perish, but have
everlasting life. (John 3.16)

Hear also what Saint Paul saith.

This is a true saying, and worthy of all men
to be received, That Christ Jesus came into
the world to save sinners. (1 Timothy 1.15)

Hear also what Saint John saith.

If any man sin, we have an Advocate with the Father, Jesus Christ the righteous; and he is the propitiation for our sins. (1 John 2.1)

Minister   Let us pray.

All   We do not presume to come to this thy table, O merciful Lord, trusting in our own righteousness, but in thy manifold and great mercies. We are not worthy so much as to gather up the crumbs under thy table. But thou art the same Lord, whose property is always to have mercy: grant us therefore, gracious Lord, so to eat the flesh of thy dear Son Jesus Christ, and to drink his blood, that our sinful bodies may be made clean by his body, and our souls washed through his most precious blood, and that we may evermore dwell in him, and he in us. Amen.

Communion is given with these words.

The Body of our Lord Jesus Christ, which was given for thee, preserve thy body and soul unto everlasting life. Take and eat this in remembrance that Christ died for thee, and feed on him in thy heart by faith with thanksgiving.

The Blood of our Jesus Christ which was shed for thee, preserve thy body and soul unto everlasting life. Drink this in remembrance

that Christ's Blood was shed for thee, and be
thankful.

After communion, the Lord's Prayer is said.

Minister   As our Saviour Christ hath commanded and
taught us, we are bold to say:

All   **Our Father, which art in heaven,**
hallowed be thy name;
thy kingdom come,
thy will be done,
in earth as it is in heaven.
Give us this day our daily bread;
and forgive us our trespasses,
as we forgive them that trespass against us;
and lead us not into temptation,
but deliver us from evil.
For thine is the kingdom,
the power, and the glory,
for ever and ever. Amen.

Then the minister says one of these prayers.

Minister   Having now by faith received the precious
Body and Blood of Christ, let us give thanks
unto our Lord God.

Almighty and everliving God, we most
heartily thank thee, for that thou dost
vouchsafe to feed us who have duly received
these holy mysteries, with the spiritual food
of the most precious Body and Blood of thy
Son, our Saviour Jesus Christ; and dost assure
us thereby of thy favour and goodness

45

towards us; and that we are very members incorporate in the mystical body of thy Son, which is the blessed company of all faithful people; and are also heirs through hope of thy everlasting kingdom, by the merits of the most precious death and passion of thy dear Son. And we most humbly beseech thee, O heavenly Father, so to assist us with thy grace, that we may continue in that holy fellowship, and do all such good works as thou hast prepared for us to walk in; through Jesus Christ our Lord, to whom, with thee and the Holy Ghost, be all honour and glory, world without end. **Amen.**

or

Minister   O Lord, holy Father, almighty everlasting God, we humbly beseech thee that the Holy Communion of the Body and Blood of thy Son Jesus Christ our Lord may be for the salvation of soul and body to this our *brother* who hath received it; through the same Jesus Christ our Lord. **Amen.** [10]

Minister   The peace of God, which passeth all under-standing, keep *your* hearts and minds in the knowledge and love of God, and of his Son Jesus Christ our Lord; and the blessing of God Almighty, the Father, ✠ the Son, and the Holy Ghost, be upon *you* and remain with *you* always.

All   **Amen.**

Rite 2

Minister	In the name of the Father, and of the Son, and of the Holy Spirit. **Amen.**

All   **Almighty God,**
unto whom all hearts be open,
all desires known,
and from whom no secrets are hid:
cleanse the thoughts of our hearts
by the inspiration of thy Holy Spirit,
that we may perfectly love thee,
and worthily magnify thy holy name;
through Christ our Lord. Amen.

The minister says the collect. One or more readings may be used, normally including a Gospel reading. Intercessions may be made.

Minister   Seeing we have a great high priest who has passed into the heavens, Jesus the Son of God, let us draw near with a true heart, in full assurance of faith, and make our confession to our heavenly Father.

All   **Almighty God, our heavenly Father,**
we have sinned against thee,
through our own fault,
in thought, and word, and deed,
and in what we have left undone.
We are heartily sorry,
and repent of all our sins.
For thy Son our Lord Jesus Christ's sake.
forgive us all that is past;
and grant that we may serve thee in
**   newness of life,**
to the glory of thy name. Amen.

Minister	Almighty God,
	who forgives all who truly repent,
	have mercy upon *you*, ✠
	pardon and deliver *you* from all your sins,
	confirm and strengthen *you* in all goodness,
	and keep *you* in life eternal;
	through Jesus Christ our Lord. **Amen.**

All **We do not presume**
to come to this thy table, O merciful Lord,
trusting in our own righteousness,
but in thy manifold and great mercies.
We are not worthy
so much as to gather up the crumbs under
thy table.
But thou art the same Lord
whose nature is always to have mercy.
Grant us therefore, gracious Lord,
so to eat the flesh of thy dear Son Jesus
Christ
and to drink his blood,
that we may evermore dwell in him
and he in us. Amen.

*The minister may explain this ministry of communion using
any of the following words.*

My *brother* in Christ, though unable to be
physically with us as we celebrated the
Eucharist on . . ., you were with us in spirit, a
member of our community of faith. We
remembered you in our prayers as we took
bread and wine, blessed them and shared
them according to our Lord's command. And
now I bring you his body and blood that you
may join with us in holy communion.

or

The Church of God, of which we are
members, has taken bread and wine and
given thanks over them according to our
Lord's command. I bring these holy gifts that
you may share in the communion of his body
and blood. We who are many are one body,
because we all share in one bread.

Minister   As our Saviour has taught us, so we pray:

All   **Our Father, who art in heaven,**
            hallowed be thy name;
            thy kingdom come;
            thy will be done;
            on earth as it is in heaven.
            Give us this day our daily bread.
            and forgive us our trespasses,
            as we forgive those who trespass against us.
            and lead us not into temptation,
            but deliver us from evil.

            For thine is the kingdom,
            **   the power, and the glory,**
            for ever and ever. Amen.

The minister says one of these invitations:

Receive the body of our Lord Jesus Christ,
which was given for you, and his blood which
was shed for you. Take this in remembrance
that Christ died for you, and feed on him in
your heart by faith with thanksgiving.

or, if communion is given in one kind:

bread only

> Receive the body of our Lord Jesus Christ
> which was given for you. Take it in
> remembrance that Christ died for you, and
> feed on him in your heart by faith with
> thanksgiving.

wine only

> Receive the blood of our Lord Jesus Christ
> which was shed for you. Drink this in
> remembrance that Christ's blood was shed
> for you and be thankful.

or this, which may be said alone or with any of the above:

Minister   This is the Lamb of God, who takes away the
              sins of the world.
              Happy are those who are called to his supper.

**Response Lord, I am not worthy to receive you,
              but only say the word, and I shall be healed.**

Giving the consecrated bread, the minister says

> The body of Christ.

or   The body of Christ preserve your body and
              soul unto everlasting life.

or   The body of our Lord Jesus Christ, which was
              given for you, preserve your body and soul
              unto everlasting life.

Giving the consecrated wine, the minister says

> The blood of Christ.

or   The blood of Christ preserve your body and soul unto everlasting life.

or   The blood of our Lord Jesus Christ, which was shed for you, preserve your body and soul unto everlasting life.

Any of the consecrated bread or wine not needed for communion is consumed.

The following prayer or the one of those given at the end of the Prayer Book order may be said.

All   **Almighty God,**
we thank thee for feeding us
with the body and blood of thy Son
    Jesus Christ our Lord.
Through him we offer thee our souls
    and bodies
to be a living sacrifice.
Strengthen us
in the power of thy Spirit,
to live and work (*or* that we may live)
to thy praise and glory. Amen.

A lay minister concludes with the grace.

> The grace of our Lord Jesus Christ.
> and the love of God
> and the fellowship of the Holy Spirit
> be with us all evermore. **Amen.**

A priest blesses the sick person using this form or one taken from section 14.

> The blessing of God Almighty,
> the Father, ✠ the Son, and the Holy Spirit,
> be upon you and remain with you always.
> **Amen.**

Rite 3

Minister   In the name of the Father, and of the Son, and of the Holy Spirit.   **Amen.**

All   **Almighty God,**
to whom all hearts are open,
all desires known,
and from whom no secrets are hidden:
cleanse the thoughts of our hearts
by the inspiration of your Holy Spirit,
that we may perfectly love you,
and worthily magnify your holy name;
through Christ our Lord. Amen.

The minister says a collect. One or more readings may be used, normally including a gospel reading. Intercessions may be made.

Minister   Let us confess our sins, in penitence and faith, firmly resolved to keep God's commandments and to live in love and peace with all.

All	**Almighty God, our heavenly Father,**
	we have sinned against you and against our
	neighbours,
	in thought, and word, and deed,
	through negligence, through weakness,
	through our own deliberate fault.
	We are truly sorry
	and repent of all our sins.
	For the sake of your Son Jesus Christ,
	who died for us,
	forgive us all that is past;
	and grant that we may serve you in newness
	of life,
	to the glory of your name. Amen.

Minister	Almighty God,
	who forgives all who truly repent,
	have mercy upon *you*, ✠
	pardon and deliver *you* from all *your* sins,
	confirm and strengthen *you* in all goodness,
	and keep *you* in life eternal;
	through Jesus Christ our Lord. **Amen.**

All	**We do not presume**
	to come to this your table, merciful Lord,
	trusting in our own righteousness,
	but in your manifold and great mercies.
	We are not worthy
	so much as to gather up the crumbs under
	your table.
	But you are the same Lord
	whose nature is always to have mercy.
	Grant us therefore, gracious Lord,
	so to eat the flesh of your dear Son Jesus
	Christ

53

and to drink his blood,
that we may evermore dwell in him
and he in us. Amen.

The minister may explain this ministry of communion using
any of the following words.

My *brother* in Christ, though unable to be
physically with us as we celebrated the
Eucharist on . . ., you were with us in spirit, a
member of our community of faith. We
remembered you in our prayers as we took
bread and wine, blessed them and shared
them according to our Lord's command. And
now I bring you his body and blood that you
may join with us in holy communion.

or

The Church of God, of which we are
members, has taken bread and wine and
given thanks over them according to our
Lord's command. I bring these holy gifts that
you may share in the communion of his body
and blood. We who are many are one body,
because we all share in one bread.

Minister   As our Saviour taught us, so we pray.

Either version of the Lord's Prayer may be used.

All   **Our Father in**   **Our Father, who art**
                 heaven,   **in heaven,**
             hallowed be your   **hallowed be thy**
                 name,   **name;**

your kingdom come,
your will be done,
on earth as in
    heaven.
Give us today our
    daily bread.
Forgive us our
    sins
as we forgive those
    who sin against
    us.
Lead us not into
    temptation
but deliver us from
    evil.
	thy kingdom come;
	thy will be done;
	on earth as it is in
	    heaven.
	Give us this day our
	    daily bread.
	And forgive us our
	    trespasses,
	as we forgive those
	who trespass against
	    us.
	And lead us not into
	    temptation;
	but deliver us from
	    evil.

For the kingdom,
    the power, and
    the glory are
    yours
now and for ever.
Amen.
	For thine is the
	    kingdom, the
	    power, and
	    the glory,
	for ever and ever.
	Amen.

The minister says one of these invitations.

Receive the body of our Lord Jesus Christ which was given for you, and his blood which was shed for you. Take this in remembrance that Christ died for you, and feed on him in your heart by faith with thanksgiving.

or, if communion is given in one kind:

bread only

Receive the body of our Lord Jesus Christ which was given for you. Take it in remembrance that Christ died for you, and feed on him in your heart by faith with thanksgiving.

wine only

Receive the blood of our Lord Jesus Christ which was shed for you. Drink this in remembrance that Christ's blood was shed for you and be thankful.

or this, which may be said alone or with any of the above:

Jesus is the Lamb of God, who takes away the sins of the world. Happy are those who are called to his supper.

Response **Lord, I am not worthy to receive you,**
but only say the word, and I shall be healed.

Giving the consecrated bread, the minister says

The body of Christ.

or The body of Christ keep you in eternal life.

Giving the consecrated wine, the minister says

The blood of Christ.

or The blood of Christ keep you in eternal life.

Any of the consecrated bread or wine not needed for communion is consumed.

56

Either version of the following prayer may be said.

Almighty God,
we thank you for
   feeding us
with the body and
   blood of your Son
   Jesus Christ our
   Lord.
Through him we
   offer you our
   souls and bodies
   to be a living
   sacrifice.
Strengthen us
in the power of
   your Spirit
to live and work
to your praise and
   glory. Amen.

Almighty God,
we thank you for
   feeding us
with the body and
   blood of your Son
   Jesus Christ our
   Lord.
Through him we
   offer you our
   souls and bodies
   to be a living
   sacrifice.
Strengthen us
in the power of
   your Spirit
that we may live
to your praise and
   glory. Amen.

A lay minister concludes with the grace.

The grace of our Lord Jesus Christ.
and the love of God
and the fellowship of the Holy Spirit
be with us all evermore.   **Amen.**

A priest blesses the sick person using this form or one taken from section 14.

The blessing of God Almighty,
the Father, ✠ the Son, and the Holy Spirit,
be upon you and remain with you always.
                              Amen.

5 CONFESSION AND ABSOLUTION

Please read the section on confession in the Pastoral Directory before using any of these rites.

PREPARATORY PRAYERS

God of all comfort:
quieten our minds
that we may make room for your healing forgiveness;
through Jesus Christ our Lord. **Amen.** [7]

God of love and wisdom,
you know all our anxieties and fears:
grant that *N* may cast all *his* care on you,
knowing that you care for *him*,
Give *him* quietness of mind,
an unshaken trust in you,
and keep *him* in perfect peace;
through Jesus Christ our Lord. **Amen.** [7]

CONFESSION

The penitent begins

Bless me, for I have sinned.

The priest says

The Lord be in your heart and upon your lips that you may truly and humbly confess your sins: In the Name of the Father, ✠ and of the Son, and of the Holy Spirit.

Amen.

The penitent makes confession using any suitable form,
such as this one.

I confess to Almighty God, to his Church, and to you,
that I have sinned by my own fault in thought, word, and
deed, in things done and left undone, especially (since
my last confession which was . . . ago) . . .
For these and all my other sins which I cannot now
remember, I am truly sorry. I pray God to have mercy on
me. I firmly intend amendment of life, and I humbly beg
forgiveness of God and his Church, and ask you for
counsel, direction, and absolution.   [4]

or

Here in your presence, Father, and before your minister
I confess that I have sinned, in my thoughts, in my
    words, in my deeds,
in what I have done and in what I have failed to do;
I have sinned through negligence, through weakness,
and through my own deliberate fault.
Some of my sins I remember and here confess
(especially . . .)
and some I have forgotten.
I am truly sorry. Have mercy on me.
I am resolved to do better. Help me.   [17]

Here the priest may offer counsel, direction and comfort

The priest may say

Almighty God have mercy upon you, forgive you all your
sins, and bring you to everlasting life.   **Amen.**

or

O most merciful God, according to your great mercy
you put away the sins of all who truly repent
and remember them no more.
Look now upon your servant who earnestly desires
    pardon and forgiveness.
As *he* puts his trust entirely and only in your mercy
count not *his* sins against him.
but strengthen *him* by your Holy Spirit
and make him worthy of your heavenly kingdom,
through the merits of Jesus Christ our Lord.   **Amen.**

*The priest then declares God's forgiveness in one of these
forms.*

Our Lord Jesus Christ,
who offered himself as the perfect sacrifice to the Father,
and who conferred power on his Church to forgive sins,
absolve ✠ you through my ministry by the grace of the
    Holy Spirit,
and restore you in the perfect peace of the Church.
                                        Amen.   [4]

Our Lord Jesus Christ, who has left power to his Church
to absolve all sinners who truly repent and believe in
him, of his great mercy forgive you all your offences; and
by his authority committed to me, I absolve ✠ you from
all your sins: In the Name of the Father, and of the Son,
and the Holy Spirit.   **Amen.**   [4]

*A deacon or lay person makes a declaration of forgiveness
in these words.*

Our Lord Jesus Christ,
who offered himself to be sacrificed for us to the Father,

forgives your sins by the grace of the Holy Spirit.
Amen. [4]

Either of these prayers may be used after the absolution.

The passion of our Lord Jesus Christ, and his infinite
    merits,
supply what is wanting in this thy confession,
and be to thee for the remission of sins,
the increase of grace, and the reward of eternal life.
                                                    Amen. [14]

May the passion of our Lord Jesus Christ,
the merits of Blessed Mary Ever-Virgin and of all the
    saints,
whatsoever good thou hast done
and evil thou hast suffered
be to thee for the remission of sins
the increase of grace,
and the reward of eternal life.   **Amen.**

The priest may bless the penitent.

The blessing of God Almighty, the Father, ✠ the Son,
and the Holy Spirit, be upon you and remain with you
always. **Amen.**

The priest dismisses the penitent.

Go in peace, the Lord has put away your sin,
and pray for me, a sinner.

6 LAYING ON OF HANDS AND ANOINTING

These are forms for use at home or in hospital. In a technical sense, they are neither a form of public prayer nor the administration of a sacrament (as the official teaching of the Church of England reserves the name 'sacrament' for Baptism and the holy Eucharist). Because of this the modern language version does not follow the form provided in the ASB supplementary volume Ministry to the Sick, *and may be used instead of it.*

BLESSING OF OIL

It is preferable to use oil blessed by the bishop. If it is not available, pure olive oil may be blessed by a priest with these words (other forms are given in section 15).

O Lord, Holy Father, giver of health and salvation, send your Holy Spirit to sanctify ✠ this oil; that, as your holy apostles anointed many that were sick and healed them, so may those who in faith and repentance receive this holy unction be made whole; through Jesus Christ our Lord, who lives and reigns with you and the Holy Spirit, one God, for ever and ever. **Amen.** [4]

Either of the rites may be used. Some part of the visitation of the sick may appropriately precede the laying on of hands and anointing. If the sick person has not yet made a confession and received absolution, a penitential rite should be used.

Traditional Language Rite

ANTIPHON   O Saviour of the world, who by thy cross
and precious blood hast redeemed us,
save us and help us, we humbly beseech
thee, O Lord.

*This psalm (121) may be said, or else another psalm,
especially 23, 27, 43, 71 (verses 1–17), 77, 86, 103, 130, 142
or 146.*

PSALM 121

1   I will lift up mine eyes unto the hills;
    from whence cometh my help?
2   My help cometh even from the Lord,
    who hath made heaven and earth.
3   He will not suffer thy foot to be moved;
    and he that keepeth thee will not sleep.
4   Behold, he that keepeth Israel
    shall neither slumber nor sleep.
5   The Lord himself is thy keeper;
    the Lord is thy defence upon thy right hand;
6   So that the sun shall not burn thee by day,
    neither the moon by night.
7   The Lord shall preserve thee from all evil;
    yea, it is even he that shall keep thy soul.
8   The Lord shall preserve thy going out and thy
      coming in,
    from this time forth for evermore.

ANTIPHON   O Saviour of the world, who by thy cross
and precious blood hast redeemed us,
save us and help us, we humbly beseech
thee, O Lord.

A SHORT LESSON

James 5. 14, 15

Is any among you sick? Let him call for the elders of the church; and let them pray over him, anointing him with oil in the name of the Lord: and the prayer of faith shall save him that is sick, and the Lord shall raise him up, and if he have committed sins, it shall be forgiven him.

THE LAYING ON OF HANDS

The minister shall invite any present to pray silently, and then say

O Almighty God, whose blessed Son didst lay his hands upon the sick and heal them, grant, we beseech thee, to this thy servant on whom we now lay hands in his name, refreshment of spirit, and, according to thy gracious will, restoration to health of body and mind; through the same thy Son Jesus Christ our Lord. **Amen.**   [20]

Then shall the minister lay hands upon the head of the sick person and say

I lay my hands on thee in the name of our Saviour Jesus Christ, beseeching him that through his merits and precious death he will grant thee forgiveness of thy sins, relief from thy pain, and recovery of health in mind and body, to the glory of his name. **Amen.**   [20]

or

N, I lay my hands upon thee in the name of the Father, and of the Son, and of the Holy Ghost, beseeching our Lord Jesus Christ to sustain thee with his presence, to drive away from thee all sickness of body and spirit, and to give unto thee the victory of life and peace which will enable thee to serve him both now and evermore.

Amen. [4]

or

In the name of God most high, may release from thy
    pain be given thee,
and thy health be restored according to his holy will.
In the name of Jesus Christ, the Prince of Life,
may new life quicken thy mortal body.
In the name of the Holy Spirit,
mayest thou receive inward health,
and the peace which passeth all understanding.
And the God of all peace himself sanctify you wholly;
and may your spirit and soul and body be preserved
    entire,
without blame at the coming of our Lord Jesus Christ.

Amen. [10]

The minister may then anoint the sick person saying

N, I anoint thee in the name of the Father, and of the
    Son, and of the Holy Spirit. **Amen.**

As with this holy oil thou art outwardly anointed, so may
    our heavenly Father grant that thou mayest be
    inwardly anointed with the Holy Spirit.
May he, of his great mercy, restore unto thee health and
    strength to serve him, and send thee release from pain
    in body and mind.
May he forgive thee all thy sins, preserve thee in all
    goodness, and bring thee to everlasting life;
through Jesus Christ our Lord. **Amen.** [20]

The minister shall wipe away the oil from the forehead of the sick person and from his or her own hand using cotton wool. A period of silent prayer may be kept. Then the Lord's Prayer is said.

Our Father, which art in heaven,
hallowed be thy name;
thy kingdom come,
thy will be done,
in earth as it is in heaven.
Give us this day our daily bread;
and forgive us our trespasses,
as we forgive them that trespass against us;
and lead us not into temptation,
but deliver us from evil.
For thine is the kingdom,
the power, and the glory,
for ever and ever. Amen.

The minister may then say

The almighty Lord, who is a most strong tower to all them that put their trust in him, to whom all things in heaven, in earth, and under the earth, do bow and obey, be now and evermore thy defence, and make thee know and feel that there is none other name under heaven given to man, in whom and through whom thou mayest receive health and salvation, but only the name of our Lord Jesus Christ. **Amen.** [9]

The rites concludes with this blessing.

Unto God's gracious mercy and protection we commit
thee.
The Lord bless thee and keep thee.
The Lord make his face shine upon thee and be gracious
unto thee.
The Lord lift up his countenance upon thee, and give
thee peace,
both now and evermore. **Amen.** [9]

Modern Language Rite

This preparatory prayer may be said.

Holy Spirit, come and be with us,
guide and inspire us,
let us know your power.
Power to heal,
power to comfort,
power to console.
Holy Spirit, come and be with us. [17]

ANTIPHON   Saviour of the world, by your cross and
            precious blood you have redeemed us;
            save us and help us, we humbly beseech
            you, O Lord.

*This psalm (121) may be said, or else another psalm,
especially 23, 27, 43, 71 (verses 1–17), 77, 86, 103, 130, 142
or 146. Another version may be used; see above.*

PSALM 121

1 I lift up my eyes to the hills;
from where is my help to come?

2 My help comes from the Lord,
the maker of heaven and earth.

3 He will not let your foot be moved
and he who watches over you will not fall asleep.

4 Behold, he who keeps watch over Israel
shall neither slumber nor sleep;

5 The Lord himself watches over you;
the Lord is your shade at your right hand,

6 So that the sun shall not strike you by day,
nor the moon by night.

7 The Lord shall preserve you from all evil;
it is he who shall keep you safe.

8 The Lord shall watch over your going out and your
coming in,
from this time forth for evermore.

ANTIPHON   Saviour of the world, by your cross and
precious blood you have redeemed us;
save us and help us, we humbly beseech
you, O Lord.

A SHORT LESSON

*This lesson or some other suitable passage drawn from
section 15 may be used.*

James 5.14–16

Are any among you sick? They should call for the elders
of the church and have them pray over them, anointing
them with oil in the name of the Lord. The prayer of

faith will save the sick, and the Lord will raise them up; and anyone who has committed sins will be forgiven. Therefore confess your sins one to another, and pray for one another, so that you may be healed.

LAYING ON OF HANDS

The minister then lays hands upon the sick person, and says one of the following

N, I lay my hands upon you in the name of the Father, and of the Son, and of the Holy Spirit, beseeching our Lord Jesus Christ to sustain you with his presence, to drive away all sickness of body and spirit, and to give you that victory of life and peace which will enable you to serve him both now and evermore. **Amen.** [4]

or

N, I lay my hands upon you in the name of our Lord and Saviour Jesus Christ, beseeching him to uphold you and fill you with his grace, that you may know the healing power of his love. **Amen.** [4]

ANOINTING

If the person is to be anointed, the minister dips a thumb in the holy oil, and makes the sign of the cross on the sick person's forehead and, if desired, on their hands, saying

N, I anoint you with oil in the Name of the Father, and of the Son, and of the Holy Spirit. **Amen.**

The minister may add

As you are outwardly anointed with this holy oil, so may our heavenly Father grant you the inward anointing of the Holy Spirit. Of his great mercy, may he forgive you your sins, release you from suffering, and restore you to wholeness and strength. May he deliver you from all evil, preserve you in all goodness, and bring you to everlasting life; through Jesus Christ our Lord.
Amen. [4]

After the anointing, the minister may say one of these prayers:

God our healer,
keep us aware of your presence,
support us with your power,
comfort us with your protection,
give us strength
and establish us in your peace.   [8]

or

God of mercy, source of all healing,
we give you thanks for your gifts of strength and life,
and especially for the gift of your Son, Jesus Christ,
through whom we have health and salvation.
Help us by your Holy Spirit to feel your power in our
  lives
and to know your eternal love;
through Jesus Christ our Lord. **Amen.** [6]

Minister   As our Saviour has taught us, so we pray

Either version of the Lord's Prayer may be used.

All	**Our Father in heaven,**	**Our Father, who art in heaven,**

All

Our Father in heaven,
hallowed be your name,
your kingdom come,
your will be done,
on earth as in heaven.
Give us today our daily bread.
Forgive us our sins
as we forgive those who sin against us.
Lead us not into temptation
but deliver us from evil.

For the kingdom, the power, and the glory are yours
now and for ever. Amen.

Our Father, who art in heaven,
hallowed be thy name;
thy kingdom come;
thy will be done;
on earth as it is in heaven.
Give us this day our daily bread.
And forgive us our trespasses,
as we forgive those who trespass against us.
And lead us not into temptation;
but deliver us from evil.

For thine is the kingdom, the power, and the glory,
for ever and ever. Amen.

The Minister may conclude with these words.

The almighty Lord, who is a strong tower to all who put their trust in him, to whom all things in heaven, on earth, and under the earth bow and obey, be now and evermore your defence, and make you know and feel that the only name under heaven given for health and salvation is the name of our Lord Jesus Christ.
Amen.   [9 altered]

The Minister may say this or another blessing.

The blessing of God Almighty, the Father, ✠ and Son, and the Holy Spirit be upon you and remain with you always. **Amen.**

7 RITES WITH THE DYING

It may be appropriate to use the rites for anointing and for giving holy communion in addition to this rite.

Minister   Almighty God, look on this your servant, lying in great weakness, and comfort *him* with the promise of life everlasting, given in the resurrection of your Son Jesus Christ our Lord. **Amen.** [4]

The minister may sprinkle the sick person, the person's bed and those gathered, with holy water, saying

Sprinkle me, O Lord, with hyssop, and I shall be purified; wash me, and I shall be whiter than snow.

The minister may present an image of Christ crucified to the sick person and may light a candle or employ other devotional aids. When possible, it is desirable that members of the family and friends come together to join in this litany.

Minister   God the Father,

All   **Have mercy on your servant.**

Minister   God the Son,

All   **Have mercy on your servant.**

Minister   God the Holy Spirit,

All   **Have mercy on your servant.**

Minister	Holy Trinity, one God,
All	**Have mercy on your servant.**

Minister	Look with mercy on your servant, and in your loving mercy
All	**Good Lord, deliver *him*.**
Minister	From all evil, from all sin, from all tribulation,
All	**Good Lord, deliver *him*,**
Minister	From darkness and doubt,
All	**Good Lord, deliver *him*,**
Minister	By your holy incarnation, by your cross and passion, by your precious death and burial,
All	**Good Lord, deliver *him*,**
Minister	By your glorious resurrection and ascension, and by the coming of the Holy Spirit,
All	**Good Lord, deliver *him*,**

Minister	We sinners beseech you to hear us, Lord Christ: that it may please you to grant *him* relief in pain.
All	**We beseech you to hear us, good Lord.**
Minister	That it may please you to deliver the soul of your servant from the power of evil, and from eternal death.
All	**We beseech you to hear us, good Lord.**
Minister	That it may please you mercifully to pardon all *his* sins.

All	**We beseech you to hear us, good Lord.**
Minister	That it may please you to grant *him* a place of refreshment and everlasting blessedness.
All	**We beseech you to hear us, good Lord.**
Minister	That it may please you to give *him* joy and gladness in your kingdom, with your saints in light.
All	**We beseech you to hear us, good Lord.**
Minister	Son of God,
All	**We beseech you to hear us, good Lord.**

Minister	Jesus, Lamb of God:
All	**Have mercy on *him*.**
Minister	Jesus, bearer of our sins:
All	**Have mercy on *him*.**
Minister	Jesus, redeemer of the world:
All	**Give *him* your peace.**

Minister	Lord, have mercy.
All	**Christ, have mercy.**
Minister	Lord, have mercy. [4]

Our Father in heaven,	**Our Father, who art in heaven,**
hallowed be your name,	**hallowed be thy name;**
your kingdom come,	**thy kingdom come;**
your will be done,	**thy will be done;**
on earth as in heaven.	**on earth as it is in heaven.**
Give us today our daily bread.	**Give us this day our daily bread.**
Forgive us our sins	**And forgive us our trespasses,**
as we forgive those who sin against us.	**as we forgive those who trespass against us.**
Lead us not into temptation	**And lead us not into temptation;**
but deliver us from evil.	**but deliver us from evil.**
For the kingdom, the power, and the glory are yours	**For thine is the kingdom, the power, and the glory,**
now and for ever. Amen.	**for ever and ever. Amen.**

One of these prayers may be said.

Minister   Let us pray.

Deliver your servant *N*, O Sovereign Lord
Christ, from all evil, and set *her* free from

every bond; that *she* may rest with all your
saints in the eternal habitations; where with
the Father and the Holy Spirit you live and
reign, one God, for ever and ever.
Amen. [4]

or

O Lord, your servant N has come to the end
   of *his* life.
May your holy angels now receive *him*;
may *he* come to Paradise this day;
far from pain, and struggle, and tears,
may *he* find peace and dwell with you for
ever. **Amen.**

or, if it be a child who is dying

O Lord Jesus Christ, the only-begotten Son of God,
for our sake you became a babe in Bethlehem.
We commit to your loving care this child whom you
   have called to yourself.
Send your holy angel to lead *her* gently to those
   heavenly dwelling places where the souls of those
   who sleep in you
have perpetual peace and joy; and fold *her* in the
everlasting arms of your unfailing love;
for you live and reign with the Father and the Holy
   Spirit,
one God, for ever and ever. **Amen.** [18 adapted]

*When the minister judges that death is near, one of the
following versions of the commendation may be said.*

Depart, O Christian soul, out of this world;
in the name of God the Father Almighty who created
you;
in the name of Jesus Christ who redeemed you;
in the name of the Holy Spirit who sanctifies you.
May your rest be this day in peace,
and your dwelling place in the Paradise of God.   [4]

Go forth upon your journey from this world, O Christian
soul,
in the name of God the Father almighty who created
you;
in the name of Jesus Christ who suffered for you;
in the name of the Holy Spirit, who strengthens you;
in communion with the blessed saints,
and aided by angels and archangels, and all the armies
of the heavenly host.
May your portion this day be in peace,
and your dwelling the heavenly Jerusalem.   [18 adapted]

Go forth upon thy journey, Christian soul!
Go from this world! Go, in the name of God
The Omnipotent Father, who created thee!
Go, in the Name of Jesus Christ, our Lord,
Son of the living God, who bled for thee!
Go, in the Name of the Holy Spirit, who
Hath been poured out on thee! Go, in the name
Of Angels and Archangels; in the name
Of Thrones and Dominations; in the name
Of Princedoms and of Powers; and in the name
Of Cherubim and Seraphim, go forth!
Go, in the name of Patriarchs and Prophets;
And of Apostles and Evangelists,
Of Martyrs and Confessors; in the name

Of holy Monks and Hermits; in the name
Of holy Virgins; and all Saints of God,
Both men and women, go! Go on thy course;
And may thy dwelling today be found in peace,
And may thy dwelling be the Holy Mount
Of Sion; through the Same, through Christ our Lord. [15]

*When a life-support system is withdrawn, this prayer
may be said.*

God of compassion and love,
you have breathed into us the breath of life
and have given us the exercise of our minds and wills.
In our frailty we surrender all life to you from whom it
    came,
trusting in your gracious promises;
through Jesus Christ our Lord. **Amen.**

The dying person may be addressed in these words.

N, our companion in faith and *sister* in Christ,
we entrust you to God who created you.
May you return to him who formed you from the dust of
    the earth.
May the angels and the saints come to meet you
as you go forth from this life.
May Christ, who was crucified for you,
take you into his kingdom.
May Christ, the Good Shepherd,
give you a place within his flock.
May he forgive you your sins
and keep you among his people.
May you see your Redeemer face to face
and delight in the vision of God for ever. **Amen.**

Either of these versions of the Nunc Dimittis may be said.

Lord, now lettest thou thy servant depart in peace:	Lord, now you let your servant go in peace:
according to thy word.	your word has been fulfilled.
For mine eyes have seen thy salvation,	My own eyes have seen the salvation
which thou hast prepared before the face of all people;	which you have prepared in the sight of every people;
To be a light to lighten the Gentiles,	A light to reveal you to the nations
and to be the glory of thy people Israel.	and the glory of your people Israel.

This commendatory prayer may be said.

Into your hands, O merciful Saviour, we commend your servant N. Acknowledge, we humbly beseech you, a sheep of your own fold, a lamb of your flock, a sinner of your own redeeming. Receive *him* into the arms of your mercy, into the blessed rest of everlasting peace, and into the glorious company of the saints in light.   **Amen.**   [4]

After death, the following may be said.

Come to *her* aid, O saints of God;
come forth to meet *her*, angels of the Lord;
receiving *her* soul,
presenting it to the Most High.

May Christ, who has called you, now receive you,
and may the angels bring you to Abraham's bosom.

Rest eternal grant to *her*, O Lord,
and let light perpetual shine upon *her*.

May *her* soul and the souls of all the departed,
through the mercy of God, rest in peace.   **Amen.**

This thanksgiving or something similar may be said.

We give thanks to you, Lord our God,
for the life of your servant *N*,
who has now passed from this world.
We thank you for . . .
We are glad that we shared some part of *his* life
and now entrust *him* to you,
O God of the living and the dead.   **Amen.**   [17]

8 FURTHER PRAYERS AFTER DEATH

'And when human hearts are breaking, under sorrow's iron rod, then we find that self same aching deep within the heart of God.'

(Bishop Timothy Rees)

Father of all,
we pray to you for those we love, but see no longer.
Grant them your peace; let light perpetual shine upon
them;
and in your loving wisdom and almighty power, work in
them the good purpose of your perfect will;
through Jesus Christ our Lord. **Amen.** [2]

AFTER RELEASE FROM SUFFERING

We thank you, loving Father,
for taking *N* from sickness into health,
and from suffering into joy.
Grant that those whom *she* has left
may be strengthened by your continuing presence,
and share with *her* your gift of eternal life. **Amen.**

AFTER SUDDEN DEATH

O Lord, before you brought us into this world, you
knew us.
You knew the number of days this *man* would live,
but you hid it from us for your own good purposes.

What is sudden to us was known to you before it came
    to be.
Help us to accept it and to bear it in your strength that
    your name may be glorified and your people
    sustained;
through Jesus Christ our Lord.   **Amen.**   [17]

O Lord, hear us in our pain and anguish
now that *N* has gone from us.
We are bewildered and confused;
let us find rest in you.
Help us to acknowledge and accept what has happened
and to bear it in your strength.   **Amen.**   [17]

AFTER A SUICIDE

Lord Jesus Christ,
you knew the agony of the garden and the loneliness of
    the cross,
but remained in the love of your Father.
We commend *N* to your mercy and, claiming no
    judgement for ourselves,
commit *her* to you, the righteous judge of all,
now and for ever.   **Amen.**   [17]

Compassionate God,
we entrust into your care *N*,
who has died by *his* own hand.
Grant that the knowledge of your love and mercy may
    comfort those who grieve for *him.*
Strengthen our assurance of your redeeming purpose for
    all your children,
through Jesus Christ your Son.   **Amen.**   [7]

Lord Jesus Christ,
you knew the agony of dying alone and abandoned.
We cannot know the agony which led N to take *her* own
    life.
We grieve that we could not meet *her* needs.
Console us in the face of death's seeming triumph,
    forgive us for failing N in *her* time of need,
    and give us the assurance that you can bring hope
    in our pain. **Amen.** [7]

WHEN A CHILD IS STILL-BORN

O Lord Jesus Christ, conceived by the Holy Spirit,
born of the Virgin Mary, and laid in the manger,
look with mercy on your servant in her loss.
Give her comfort in her sorrow
and hope in her desolation;
restore her to fullness of health.
We ask this for your tender mercy's sake. **Amen.** [17]

FOLLOWING THE DEATH OF A CHILD AT BIRTH

The child may be anointed during this prayer.

Lord of all, we thank you
for your work in creation,
for nourishing life in the womb,
for your love even in death.
Thank you for the life of this child N (*or* we now
    name N)
whom you gave to us and have taken to yourself.
Thank you for the arms of your love
embracing both us and N in your family.
Thank you for your presence in our sorrow.

Take our sadness, and fill us with your Spirit
to serve you on earth, and join your saints in glory,
through Jesus Christ our Lord.   **Amen.**   [17]

O Lord, hold this sweet and lovely child in your hands,
hands that show the marks of nails,
hands that know our pain.
Hold us too (especially N and N),
put your arms of love around us,
hold us tight,
for we need your support today
as we return this little one to you.   **Amen.**   [17]

Jesus,
you knew a mother's love,
you knew a father's care,
be with N and N in their loss today,
for you can withstand their anger,
wipe their tears,
comfort and console them
because you are not a stranger
but one who knows them and loves them.   **Amen.**   [17]

9 COMFORTING THE BEREAVED: PRAYERS FOR A VIGIL

When family and friends gather prior to the funeral, whether at home, in the funeral home or at church, it is appropriate to use readings, psalms and prayers. The following may be used.

Minister   Dear Friends: It was our Lord Jesus himself who said, 'Come to me, all you who labour and are burdened, and I will give you rest.' Let us pray, then, for our *brother N*, that *he* may rest from *his* labours, and enter into the light of God's eternal sabbath rest.

Receive, O Lord, your servant, for *he* returns to you.

All   **Into your hands, O Lord, we commend our *brother N*.**

Minister   Wash *him* in the holy font of everlasting life, and clothe *him* in *his* heavenly wedding garment.

All   **Into your hands, O Lord, we commend our *brother N*.**

Minister   May *he* hear your words of invitation, 'Come, you blessed of my Father'.

All   **Into your hands, O Lord, we commend our *brother N*.**

| Minister | May *he* gaze upon you, Lord, face to face, and taste the blessedness of perfect rest. |
| **All** | **Into your hands, O Lord, we commend our *brother N.*** |

| Minister | May angels surround *him,* and saints welcome *him* in peace. |
| **All** | **Into your hands, O Lord, we commend our *brother N.*** [4] |

The minister concludes with one of these prayers.

Almighty God, our Father in heaven, before whom live all who die in the Lord: Receive our *sister N* into the courts of your heavenly dwelling place. Let *her* heart and soul now ring out in joy to you, O Lord, the living God, and the God of those who live. This we ask through Christ our Lord. **Amen.** [4]

We give *her* back to thee, dear Lord, who gavest *her*
  to us.
Yet, as thou dost not lose *her* in giving,
so we have not lost *her* by his return.
Not as the world giveth, givest thou, O Lover of Souls.
What thou gavest, thou takest not away;
for what is thine, is ours also, if we are thine.
And life is eternal and love is immortal.
And death is only an horizon,
and an horizon is nothing save the limit of our sight.
Lift us up, strong Son of God, that we may see further.
Cleanse our eyes that we may see more clearly.
Draw us closer to thyself,
  that we may know ourselves nearer to our beloved
  who is with thee.

And while thou dost prepare a place for us,
prepare us too for that happy place,
that where *she* is, and thou art, we too may be.
Through Jesus Christ our Lord. **Amen.**

PRAYERS FOR THOSE WHO MOURN

Almighty God, look with pity upon the sorrows of your
servants for whom we pray. Remember them, Lord, in
mercy; nourish them with patience; comfort them with a
sense of your goodness; lift up your countenance upon
them; and give them peace; through Jesus Christ our
Lord. **Amen.** [4]

O God, whose ways are hidden and thy works most
    wonderful,
who makest nothing in vain and lovest all that thou hast
    made;
comfort thou thy servants,
    and grant that they may so love and serve thee in this
    life,
that they obtain the fulness of thy promises in the world
    to come;
through Jesus Christ our Lord. **Amen.** [18 adapted]

Almighty God, Father of mercies and giver of comfort;
deal graciously, we pray, with all who mourn;
that, casting all their care on thee,
    they may know the consolation of your love;
through Jesus Christ our Lord. **Amen.** [4]

10 EMERGENCY BAPTISM

Read the Pastoral Directory before administering this rite.

Water will be needed for the baptism. In clinical circumstances, the minister should seek advice from a doctor or nurse as to the best way to administer the sacrament. While it is usual to pour water on the head, some other part of the body (e.g. a hand or foot} may be used.

The baptism of an adult may be preceded by an affirmation of faith (see section 1).

The minister asks the name of the person to be baptized, and pours water on him *saying:*

N, I baptize you in the name of the Father, and of the Son, and of the Holy Spirit. **Amen.**

The minister says at least the Lord's Prayer. Either version may be used.

Our Father in heaven, **hallowed be your name, your kingdom come, your will be done, on earth as in heaven. Give us today our daily bread.**	**Our Father, who art in heaven, hallowed be thy name; thy kingdom come; thy will be done; on earth as it is in heaven. Give us this day our daily bread.**

Forgive us our sins	And forgive us our traspasses,
as we forgive those who sin against us.	as we forgive those who trespass against us.
Lead us not into temptation	And lead us not into temptation;
but deliver us from evil.	but deliver us from evil.
For the kingdom, the power, and the glory are yours	For thine is the kingdom, the power, and the glory,
now and for ever.	for ever and ever.
Amen.	**Amen.**

Other prayers, such as the following, may be added.

Heavenly Father, we thank you that by water and the
    Holy Spirit
you have bestowed upon this your servant the
    forgiveness of sin
and have raised *her* to the new life of grace.
Strengthen *her*, O Lord, with your presence,
enfold *her* in the arms of your mercy,
and keep *her* safe for ever. **Amen.**

The baptism ends with this blessing.

God the Father, God the Son, God the Holy Spirit,
bless, ✠ preserve, and keep you, this day and evermore.
                                                Amen.

11 BLESSINGS OF WATER, OIL, PERSONS, AND HOMES

Blessing of Water

Either form may be used. The first is a traditional rite, both in language and form, requiring salt and water to be blessed and mingled. The second is a simple blessing.

TRADITIONAL FORM

Minister	Our help is in the name of the Lord;
All	**Who hath made heaven and earth.**

The minister blesses the salt.

Almighty and everlasting God, we humbly beseech thee of thy bountiful goodness to ✠ bless and ✠ sanctify this creature of salt, which thou hast created for the use of mankind; grant that it may avail for health both of soul and body, and that whatever is touched or sprinkled therewith may be cleansed from all defilement, and defended from every assault of the evil one; through Jesus Christ our Lord. **Amen.**

Then the minister blesses the water, saying

O God, who in ordaining the sacrament of our new birth hast employed the element of water: Hear our prayers, we beseech thee, and pour upon this water the might of thy ✠ blessing, that it may serve thy gracious purpose in casting out devils and healing disease. Grant that whatever in the homes and dwelling places of thy children is sprinkled therewith may be free from all that defiles or causes hurt. Suffer not the breath of pestilence to abide therein; cast out all the snares of Satan, and drive far off every evil spirit that would trouble the peace of thy faithful people. Let all who use this water and call upon thy name be defended from every assault of evil; through Jesus Christ our Lord. **Amen.**

Here the minister shall cast the salt into the water in the form of a cross, saying

Let this mixture of salt and water be made in the name of the Father, and of the Son, and of the Holy Spirit. **Amen.**

Minister The Lord be with you.

All   **And with thy spirit.**

Minister Let us pray.

O God, the eternal King whom none may overcome, before whom the powers of darkness quail and flee: we humbly pray thee to ✠ bless this thy creature of salt and water, that wherever it is sprinkled by those who put their trust in thee, thy servants may be

delivered from the snares of the devil, and
may ever rejoice in the blessed peace of thy
Holy Spirit; through Jesus Christ our Lord.
Amen. [11]

SIMPLE FORM

God our Father, your gift of water brings life
　　and freshness to the earth,
it washes away our sins and brings eternal
　　life.
Bless and hallow ✠ this water, renew the
　　living spring of your life within us,
and protect us in spirit and body, that we
　　may be free from sin
and serve you in purity of heart;
　　through Christ our lord **Amen.** [16]

Blessing of Oil

*For anointing the sick it is preferable to use oil blessed by the
bishop. If it is not available, pure olive oil may be blessed by
a priest with these words.*

O Lord, Holy Father, giver of health and salvation,
send your Holy Spirit to sanctify ✠ this oil;
that, as your holy apostles anointed many that were sick
　　and healed them,
so may those who in faith and repentance receive this
　　holy unction be made whole;
through Jesus Christ our Lord, who lives and reigns with
　　you and the Holy Spirit,
one God, for ever and ever. **Amen.** [4]

or

God of healing and hope,
your Son our Saviour sent his disciples
to anoint the sick with oil;
fulfil your promise through this oil
which we set apart in his name
to be used as a sign of forgiveness,
healing and salvation. **Amen.**   [8]

or

O almighty God, who hast taught us in thy holy Word to
pray for the sick and anoint them with oil, that they may
recover their bodily health; Sanctify ✠, we beseech thee,
this thy creature of oil; and grant that those who shall be
anointed therewith may receive healing of body and
mind, and strengthening of spirit; through Jesus Christ
our Lord. **Amen.**   [20]

Blessings of Persons

For a simple laying-on of hands

The grace of the Lord Jesus flow forth upon thee
for the healing of soul and mind and body,
upon whom we now lay hands in his most holy name.
Amen.   [10]

For use by a lay minister.

Our Lord Jesus Christ be with you to defend you,
within you to keep you,

before you to lead you,
beside you to guide you,
and above you to bless you.   **Amen.**   [8]

Now may our Lord Jesus Christ himself and God our
    Father,
who loved us and gave us eternal comfort and good hope
    through grace,
comfort your heart and establish you in every good
    work and deed.   **Amen.**

For use by a priest

May God the Father bless you.
God the Son heal you.
God the Holy Spirit give you strength.
May God the holy and undivided Trinity
guard your body, save your soul,
and bring you to his heavenly country;
where he lives and reigns for ever and ever.   **Amen.**   [4]

God be your comfort, your strength;
God be your hope and support;
God be your light and your way;
and the blessing of God,
Creator, Redeemer and Giver of life,
remain with you now and for ever.   **Amen.**   [8]

The Lord bless you and keep you;
the Lord make his face to shine upon you and be
    gracious to you;
the Lord look kindly on you and give you peace;
and the blessing of God almighty,
the Father, ✠ the Son and the Holy Spirit,
be among you and remain with you always.   **Amen.**

or

Unto God's gracious mercy and protection we commit
    thee.
The Lord bless thee and keep thee;
the Lord make his face shine upon thee and be gracious
    unto thee;
the Lord lift up his countenance upon thee, and give
    thee peace,
both now and evermore.   **Amen.**

BLESSING OF A HOME

A PRAYER TO BANISH EVIL

*This prayer may be used alone or in conjunction with any
others given here and may be accompanied by sprinkling
with blessed water.*

> Let the mighty power of the Holy God be
> present in this place
> > to banish from it every unclean spirit,
> > to cleanse it from every residue of evil,
> > and to make it a secure habitation for
> > those who dwell in it;
> in the Name of Jesus Christ our Lord.
> **Amen.**   [19]

A SHORT BLESSING

Minister   By the mystery of thy holy incarnation;
All   **Jesu, bless this house.**

Minister   By thy Nativity at Bethlehem;
All   **Jesu, bless this house.**

Minister	By thy life in thy home at Nazareth;
All	**Jesu, bless this house.**
Minister	By the presence at the marriage in Cana;
All	**Jesu, bless this house.**
Minister	By thy visit to Zacchaeus;
All	**Jesu, bless this house.**
Minister	By thy love of the home at Bethany;
All	**Jesu, bless this house.** [11]

Minister   Let us ask God to bless this house.

Jesus, King of love, who shared in the life of
   an earthly home
with Mary and Joseph at Nazareth.
Bless, we pray thee, this house and those who
   live here.
May they live in love one with another
and welcome others in thy name
until they come to thy heavenly dwelling.
This we ask in thy name and for thy sake.
Amen.

Minister   God the Father lovingly enfold you,
God the Son grace your home and table,
God the Holy Spirit crown you with joy and
   peace.
The Lord bless you and keep you in eternal
   life. **Amen.**

12 READINGS, COLLECTS
   AND PSALMS

*These sets of readings are provided for convenience and may
be used according to pastoral necessity. Suggestions are given
for the appropriateness of various combinations but these are
only suggestions and others may be freely used. All the
readings are deliberately short and, particularly in prolonged
and chronic illness, it may be better to use the readings set
in the lectionary for the day. Special sets of readings could
also be devised for the seasons of Christmas, Easter and
Pentecost.*

Set 1: From the Book of Common Prayer

COLLECT

Almighty, everliving God, Maker of mankind,
who dost correct those whom thou dost love,
and chastise everyone whom thou dost receive;
we beseech thee to have mercy upon this thy servant
    visited with thine hand,
and to grant that *she* may take *her* sickness patiently,
and recover *her* bodily health (if it be thy gracious will,)
and whensoever *her* soul shall depart from the body,
it may be without spot presented unto thee;
through Jesus Christ our Lord. **Amen.**   [9]

Hebrews 12.5

My son, despise not thou the chastening of the Lord, nor faint when thou art rebuked of him. For whom the Lord loveth he chasteneth; and scourgeth every son whom he receiveth.

GOSPEL

John 5.24

Verily, verily I say unto you, he that heareth my word, and believeth on him that sent me, hath everlasting life, and shall not come into condemnation; but is passed from death unto life.

Set 2: From *The Priest's Vade Mecum*

COLLECT

O God, who alone canst strengthen the weakness of
  man,
show forth thy mighty help unto this thy sick servant,
that by thy merciful aid *he* may be restored whole to thy
  Church;
through Jesus Christ our Lord. **Amen.** [10]

EPISTLE

1 John 3.21, 22

Beloved, if our heart condemn us not, then have we confidence towards God. And whatsoever we ask, we

receive of him, because we keep his commandments,
and do those things that are pleasing in his sight.

GOSPEL

John 6.56–8

Jesus said, he that eateth my flesh, and drinketh my
blood, dwelleth in me, and I in him. As the living Father
hath sent me, and I live by the Father: so he that eateth
me, even he shall live by me. This is that bread which
came down from heaven: not as your fathers did eat
manna, and are dead: he that eateth of this bread shall
live for ever.

Set 3: An Alternative Traditional Set

COLLECTS

Almighty Father, giver of life and health,
look mercifully, we beseech thee, on this thy servant,
that by thy blessing upon *him* and upon those who
    minister to *him*,
he may speedily be restored to health, if it be thy
    gracious will,
and live to the glory of thy holy name;
through Jesus Christ our Lord. **Amen.**   [18]

or

Assist us mercifully, O Lord, in these our supplications
    and prayers,
and dispose the way of thy servant towards the
    attainment of everlasting salvation;

that among all the changes and chances of this mortal
  life,
he may ever be defended by thy most gracious and ready
  help;
through Jesus Christ our Lord. **Amen.**   [18]

EPISTLE

2 Corinthians 1.3

Blessed be God, even the Father of our Lord Jesus Christ,
the Father of mercies, and the God of all comfort; who
comforteth us in all our tribulation, that we may be able
to comfort them which are in any trouble, by the comfort
with wherewith we ourselves are comforted of God.
For as the sufferings of Christ abound in us, so our
consolation also aboundeth by Christ.

GOSPEL

John 10.15, 27–30

I am the good shepherd; and I know mine own, and
mine own know me, even as the Father knoweth me,
and I know the Father; and I lay down my life for the
sheep. My sheep hear my voice, and I know them, and
they follow me: and I give unto them eternal life; and
they shall never perish, and no one shall pluck them out
of my hand. My father, which hath given them unto me,
is greater than all; and no one is able to pluck them out
of the Father's hand. I and the Father are one.

Set 4: For use with the sick
(suitable for an occasional home communion)

COLLECT

God of grace, power, and mercy;
look on your servant *N* with compassion,
give *her* courage and complete confidence in your
    protection,
and keep *her* in peace,
through Jesus Christ our Lord. **Amen.**

or

Almighty God,
you know that we have no power of ourselves to help
    ourselves:
keep us both outwardly in our bodies and inwardly in
    our souls,
that we may be defended from all adversities which may
    happen to the body,
and from all evil thoughts which may assault and hurt
    the soul;
through Jesus Christ our Lord,
who lives and reigns with you and the Holy Spirit,
one God, for ever and ever. **Amen.**   [4]

EPISTLE

Philippians 4.4–7 (RSV)

Rejoice in the Lord always; again I will say, Rejoice. Let
all men know your forbearance. The Lord is at hand.
Have no anxiety about anything, but in everything by
prayer and supplication with thanksgiving let your

requests be made known to God. And the peace of God, which passes all understanding, will keep your hearts and your minds in Christ Jesus.

or

Hebrews 4.14–16 (NRSV)

Since, then, we have a great high priest who has passed through the heavens, Jesus, the Son of God, let us hold fast to our confession. For we do not have a high priest who is unable to sympathize with our weaknesses, but we have one who in every respect has been tested as we are, yet without sin. Let us therefore approach the throne of grace with boldness, so that we may receive mercy and find grace to help in time of need.

or

1 John 5.13–15 (NRSV)

I write these things to you who believe in the name of the Son of God, so that you may know that you have eternal life. And this is the boldness we have in him, that if we ask anything according to his will, he hears us. And if we know that he hears us in whatever we ask, we know that we have obtained the requests made of him.

GOSPEL

John 6.47–51 (NRSV)

Jesus said: 'Very truly, I tell you, whoever believes has eternal life. I am the bread of life. Your ancestors ate the manna in the wilderness, and they died. This is the bread

that comes down from heaven, so that one may eat of it
and not die. I am the living bread that came down from
heaven. Whoever eats of this bread will live forever; and
the bread that I will give for the life of the world is my
flesh.'

Set 5: For use when anointing is to be given

COLLECT

Heavenly Father,
you anointed your Son Jesus Christ with the Holy Spirit
    and with power
to bring us the blessings of your kingdom.
Grant that we, who share in his sufferings and victory
may receive the benefits of his anointing;
who lives and reigns with you and the Holy Spirit,
one God, for ever and ever. **Amen.**   [1 adapted]

EPISTLE

James 5.14–16 (NRSV)

Are any among you sick? They should call for the elders
of the church and have them pray over them, anointing
them with oil in the name of the Lord. The prayer of
faith will save the sick, and the Lord will raise them up;
and anyone who has committed sins will be forgiven.
Therefore confess your sins to one another, and pray for
one another, so that you may be healed. The prayer of
the righteous is powerful and effective.

GOSPEL

Mark 6.7, 12–13 (NRSV)

Jesus called the twelve and began to send them out two
by two, and gave them authority over the unclean spirits.
So they went out and proclaimed that all should repent.
They cast out many demons, and anointed with oil many
who were sick and cured them.

THE PSALMS

*The Psalms form a great treasury of material for providing
comfort and encouragement as well as for expressing
penitence, anger and despondency. They are frequently better
known in the Coverdale Psalter version than in the form
found in the various translations of the Bible. Here the
Coverdale version and the American Prayer Book version
have both been used (and Psalm 23 is given in its familiar
metrical version).*

PENITENCE AND FORGIVENESS

PSALM 6

1 Lord, do not rebuke me in your anger;
   do not punish me in your wrath.
2 Have pity on me, Lord, for I am weak;
   heal me, Lord, for my bones are racked.
3 My spirit shakes with terror;
   how long, O Lord, how long?
4 Turn, O Lord, and deliver me;
   save me for your mercy's sake.

5　For in death no one remembers you;
　　and who will give you thanks in the grave?
6　I grow weary because of my groaning;
　　every night I drench my bed
　　　and flood my couch with tears.
7　My eyes are wasted with grief
　　and worn away because of all my enemies.
8　Depart from me, all evildoers,
　　for the Lord has heard the sound of my weeping.
9　The Lord has heard my supplication;
　　the Lord accepts my prayer.
10　All my enemies shall be confounded and quake
　　　with fear;
　　they shall turn back and suddenly be put to shame.

PSALM 32

1　Blessed is he whose unrighteousness is forgiven:
　　and whose sin is covered.
2　Blessed is the man unto whom the Lord imputeth
　　　no sin:
　　and in whose spirit there is no guile.
3　For while I held my tongue:
　　my bones consumed away through my daily
　　　complaining.
4　For thy hand is heavy upon me day and night:
　　and my moisture is like the drought in summer.
5　I will acknowledge my sin unto thee:
　　and mine unrighteousness have I not hid.
6　I said, I will confess my sins unto the Lord:
　　and so thou forgavest the wickedness of my sin.
7　For this shall every one that is godly make his prayer
　　　unto thee, in a time when thou mayest be found:

but in the great water-floods they shall not come
   nigh him.
8 Thou art a place to hide me in, thou shalt preserve
   me from trouble:
   thou shalt compass me about with songs of
   deliverance.
9 I will inform thee, and teach thee in the way wherein
   thou shalt go:
   and I will guide thee with mine eye.
10 Be ye not like to horse and mule, which have no
   understanding:
   whose mouths must be held with bit and bridle, lest
   they fall upon thee.
11 Great plagues remain for the ungodly:
   but whoso putteth his trust in the Lord, mercy
   embraceth him on every side.
12 Be glad, O ye righteous, and rejoice in the Lord:
   and be joyful, all ye that are true of heart.   [9]

Psalms 51, 130 and 143 are also suitable.

ENCOURAGEMENT

PSALM 18.1–6

1 I will love thee, O Lord, my strength;
   the Lord is my stony rock, and my defence:
   my saviour, my God, and my might, in whom I will
   trust,
   my buckler, the horn also of my salvation, and my
   refuge.
2 I will call upon the Lord, which is worthy to be raised:
   so shall I be safe from mine enemies.

3   The sorrows of death compassed me:
    and the overflowings of ungodliness made me afraid.
4   The pains of hell came about me:
    the snares of death overtook me.
5   In my trouble I will call upon the Lord:
    and complain unto my God.
6   So shall he hear my voice out of his holy temple:
    and my complaint shall come before him, it shall
        enter even into his ears.

PSALM 62. 1–2, 6–9, 13–14

1   For God alone my soul in silence waits;
    from him comes my salvation.
2   He alone is my rock and my salvation,
    my stronghold, so that I shall not be greatly shaken.
6   For God alone my soul in silence waits;
    truly, my hope is in him.
7   He alone is my rock and my salvation,
    my stronghold, so that I shall not be shaken.
8   In God is my safety and my honour;
    God is my strong rock and my refuge.
9   Put your trust in him always, O people,
    pour out your hearts before him, for God is our
        refuge.
13 God has spoken once, twice have I heard it,
    that power belongs to God.
14 Steadfast love is yours, O Lord,
    for you repay everyone according to his deeds.

Psalms 13, 16, 91 and 121 are also suitable.

WHEN NEAR DEATH

PSALM 23 (METRICAL VERSION)

The Lord's my Shepherd, I'll not want;
    he makes me down to lie
In pastures green; he leadeth me
    the quiet waters by.

My soul he doth restore again,
    and me to walk doth make
Within the paths of righteousness,
    e'en for his own name's sake.

Yea, though I walk through death's dark vale,
    yet will I fear none ill;
For thou art with me, and thy rod
    and staff me comfort still.

My table thou hast furnished
    in presence of my foes;
My head thou dost with oil anoint,
    and my cup overflows.

Goodness and mercy all my life
    shall surely follow me;
And in God's house for evermore
    my dwelling-place shall be.

Psalm 25 is also suitable.

THE LOVE OF GOD

PSALM 36.5–10

5 Your love, O Lord, reaches to the heavens,
   and your faithfulness to the clouds.
6 Your righteousness is like the strong mountains,
       your justice like the great deep;
     you save both man and beast, O Lord.
7 How priceless is your love, O God!
     your people take refuge under the shadow of your
       wings.
8 They feast upon the abundance of your house;
     you give them drink from the river of your delights.
9 For with you is the well of life,
   and in your light we see light.
10 Continue your loving-kindness to those who know
       you,
     and your favour to those who are true of heart.

13 PASTORAL DIRECTORY: GUIDANCE ON VARIOUS ASPECTS OF THE RITES

Anointing

Within the catholic tradition it is anointing with oil and not the laying on of hands which may accompany anointing, which is the sacramental rite. The Church of England teaches that anointing is a ministry of the ordained priesthood, that the material element is pure olive oil which has been blessed, and that the method of administration is by anointing with oil on the forehead in the sign of the cross, and that other parts of the body may be anointed in addition. (See, however, notes on behaviour.) It is generally held that anointing should be used more sparingly than the laying on of hands and that it is especially appropriate in a crisis. Pastoral sense suggests that this rite should be available to all who need it, that it should be withheld from no one, and that it is to be preferred whenever sickness threatens the quality of life or life itself.

See also *Oils*.

Baptism

Emergency baptism of a child

The practice of baptizing children very shortly after birth is not generally maintained today and a child may be baptized weeks or months or even years after birth, or not at all. Nevertheless, in the case of serious neo-natal illness, those who would expect to have their child baptized at some later point may request an emergency baptism. The notes to the ASB provision state that 'the parents are responsible for requesting emergency baptism'. Good pastoral practice suggests that the possibility of such baptism should be put to them.

The ordinary minister would be the priest having pastoral care of the child and his or her parents, e.g. their parish priest or the hospital chaplain. In the absence of a priest or other authorized minister, any lay person may be the minister and has the responsibility of informing those with pastoral responsibility for the parents and child that the baptism has taken place. Baptism should not be administered by the minister alone with the child and there should be at least one and preferably two witnesses. To avoid all doubt they should sign a simple declaration that the child has been baptized in water in the name of the Father, Son and Holy Spirit. The baptism should then be recorded in the register of the hospital or parish. Water and no other liquid must be used for baptism. A child can be properly and validly baptized even if its name is not known. If the child lives, it is brought to church for the supplementary rites (see ASB 280, s. 110). It is contrary to Christian doctrine to baptize the dead.

Emergency baptism of an adult

The same basic rules apply to the baptism of an adult in a real emergency, e.g. where a planned baptism is prevented by sudden and serious accident or ill-health. In other situations of acute or chronic illness baptism may be administered in fuller form using a profession of faith. Under the present rules, an adult will require confirmation if he or she recovers from illness and the bishop should be informed that the baptism has taken place. Alternatively, the bishop may be available to perform the full rite at home or in hospital. In the case of real necessity, the minister should not hesitate to baptize and give communion to a seriously sick person.

Behaviour

A high standard of professional behaviour is expected from all, ordained or lay, who minister to people in situations of weakness. It is now generally acknowledged that an imbalance of power creates the possibility of exploitation and abuse. Ministers must guard against this and be careful to allow sick people their full and proper dignity, accepting their reserve in matters relating to their sickness, and respecting their physical persons. Care must be taken both over language and over gesture and touch. Only the highest possible professional standards will maintain the high regard that the faithful have for their ministers and prevent scandal. As a basic rule, the minister should always dress appropriately. In an emergency, it may be necessary to wear casual clothes, but this should be exceptional.

Pastoral care should always take place in ordinary circumstances and never be concealed or be at odd times or places. It is as well to establish what is normal pastoral behaviour by discussing it with those in authority, clerical and lay, and, in teaching or preaching about ministry to the sick, make clear what such ministry involves. If there is any doubt, ask whether something is acceptable. If the minister has any doubts or difficulties about a situation, he or she should ask another person to be present, possibly at a discrete distance. It is always better to be safe.

Chaplains, see *Hospitals and their Chaplains*

Communion of the Sick

There are three ways of providing communion for the sick at home or in hospital: first, celebration of the Holy Communion in the presence of the sick person; second, bringing communion from a celebration that has just taken place in church; third, bringing the reserved sacrament from the church.

The frequency with which a priest feels able to celebrate the Holy Communion will determine normal practice in a parish. The old rule that a priest should only celebrate once on any day has much to commend it, even though we have become used to multiple celebrations. The communion should be celebrated with attention and devotion, and this is simply not possible when celebrations are constantly multiplied. A sensible approach is for communion to be taken to the sick immediately after a celebration in church. During a prolonged illness this regular pattern would be helpfully punctuated by a celebration in the home or hospital.

The minister must judge, in conversation with the sick person, how much of a rite should be used. A recommended minimum would be a collect, confession and absolution, prayer of humble access, Lord's Prayer and blessing. Many who are unable to be present regularly in church would welcome more of the service, e.g. the *Gloria*, a prayer of thanksgiving after communion, etc.

The reserved sacrament should be taken to the sick in a seemly way. This sounds obvious but it is all too easy to put the pyx in a pocket along with one's keys! After an individual communion or the completion of a series of visits to give communion, any of the consecrated bread and wine that remains should either be consumed or taken immediately to the place of reservation.

Confession

We may differentiate between formal and informal acts of confession. Ministers, ordained and lay, often hear confessions in an informal sort of way when people, perhaps rather unexpectedly, pour out their souls. In such a situation we can listen carefully, offer advice and give assurance of God's forgiveness. We should maintain a rule of strict confidentiality about such informal outpourings, as much as we do when we hear confessions in more formal circumstances.

Formal confession is of two sorts. One is associated with public worship, when a person, after due preparation, joins in a general confession. The Anglican Church has placed great value on these public and corporate forms, but it has also allowed, in varying circumstances, another form, that of individual confession to a priest. This is not the place to discuss the theological aspects of such confession – and a good deal has been written about it – but only to provide pastoral guidance concerning the administration of confession.

Confessions are best heard in church. If you have any doubt about the propriety of hearing a particular person's confession alone try to ensure that a person of the same sex as the penitent is present in the building, though not, of course, able to hear the exchange. It is recommended that the minister wears vesture appropriate to his or her position as a priest. This would appropriately be the wearing of a purple stole over a cassock or a cassock and surplice. The priest should sit. The penitent may sit or kneel.

Using one of the forms provided, the penitent is

encouraged to express the source of guilt. As far as possible this should be expressed in the penitent's own words. The confessor may use simple prompts if the penitent is finding it difficult to make the confession but should be wary of leading questions. Above all, the confessor must be patient, listen carefully and give the penitent complete and loving attention. Great care should be exercised if sins of a sexual nature are being confessed and detailed descriptions should be curtailed (see the section on *Behaviour*).

A penitent may list certain sins as matters of fact without giving any indication of repentance and remorse. The priest cannot give absolution unless the penitent is contrite. In the absence of obvious contrition the confessor should seek for further assurances that the penitent is intent on changing the pattern of behaviour which is the source of guilt.

The penitent is able to confess to the priest with the assurance that complete confidentiality will be maintained. The confessor should not repeat the confession to any other person nor refer to the matter with the penitent except at that person's specific request. The content of a confession is not, nevertheless, normal matter for conversation between priest and penitent.

In urgent necessity, but not otherwise, a lay person or a deacon may hear a confession and use the declaration of forgiveness provided in the rite rather than give absolution.

Confidentiality

Deliberately or not, the minister will know a great deal about people which is not common knowledge. This knowledge must be treated with considerable care. The fact that someone is sick or in hospital should not be generally made known without their consent and they should be remembered in silence at the intercession. Knowledge of their personal and family circumstances should also be treated with discretion. Examples of Christian fortitude and patience are a valuable resource for preaching but again care should be taken to ensure a person's willingness to provide such an example.

Other professionals are also bound by a confidentiality that clergy may find frustrating. Nevertheless, it must be respected. When permission is given by the patient, health professionals will gladly talk with pastors, especially when they recognize the importance of the patient's faith to his or her general well-being.

See also *Hospitals and their Chaplains.*

Counselling

The minister, ordained and lay, will often be asked for counsel. As a general rule a minister should not see a person for counselling on a regular one-to-one basis on more than three occasions unless they are themselves being supervised by another professional. If in doubt about the wisdom of continuing, seek advice.

Deliverance from Evil and Exorcism

The Bible bears eloquent testimony to Christ's power with regard to evil spirits and demons. The Church has long used his authority to continue this powerful ministry. In an age which has witnessed a significant revival of occult activity there will be occasions when ministers are asked to deal with possible instances of malign spiritual interference or at least with the effects of involvement in occult practices.

Authority in all aspects of the ministry of deliverance

from evil belongs to the Bishop and no form of exorcism should be attempted without the advice of qualified advisers and the consent of the Bishop.

In a real pastoral emergency, prayer is the only resort. A minister should seek support from other ordained ministers and from mature responsible lay people with whom he or she should pray for spiritual protection.

Where people experience disturbances or a sense of evil in a dwelling place, prayers of blessing may be used and holy water may be sprinkled. Again, advice should be sought from qualified and experienced practitioners authorized by the Bishop.

Emergency Baptism, see *Baptism*

Exorcism, see *Deliverance from evil, and exorcism*

Hospitals and their Chaplains

Chaplains are partners with the parish clergy and lay ministers in the care of the sick. They welcome referrals from the parishes that enable them to make ready contact with those brought into hospital. A list of whole-time hospital chaplains is given at the back of *Crockford's Clerical Directory*. The Hospital Chaplaincies Council at Church House, Westminster (tel. 0171 222 9011) can provide details of both whole- and part-time chaplains. Chaplains will gladly and readily ensure that parishioners are brought communion or are able to come to chapel, if they desire it. Parish clergy and lay ministers are usually welcome to come into the hospital to minister to their own parishioners. It is a basic courtesy to contact the chaplain first.

Clergy and lay ministers should always check that they can visit a ward outside general visiting times and should make themselves known to ward staff on arrival. The hospital environment is increasingly high-tech. Chaplains are themselves careful to ask about any pre-conditions for going on a ward or into any special unit. The basic rule again is 'If in doubt, ask'. Failure to do so can get the clergy a bad reputation and make visiting more difficult in future.

Ministers, especially parish clergy, should stay with some of the more painful situations in hospital, alongside the chaplain, seeking advice as necessary.

Lay Ministry

Lay persons have a very important and rather undervalued role in ministry to the sick and we need to be clear both about what they can and cannot do. The first and most basic thing they can do is to uphold the sick in prayer. The second is to carry out visiting and to do so not just as individuals but specifically as representatives of the Church. Christ has laid on us all a charge to visit the sick. Some lay persons have a charism or gift of healing and may be invited by the ordained ministers, to whom pastoral care is committed, to join in the laying on of hands for healing. A lay person may baptize in an emergency. Lay persons with episcopal permission may bring the Holy Communion to the sick. Lay persons are not permitted to give absolution or a formal blessing (forms of lay blessing are given in section 13) of the sort given by a priest and they may not lawfully anoint the sick.

Laying on of Hands

Laying on of hands is a part of the Church's ministry to the sick. In an informal way anyone may lay hands upon another person and pray for them. In the formal sense, an authorized minister of the Church, ordained or lay, should perform the rite, and those lay persons who have a specific gift of healing may join in at the minister's invitation. Many who have little experience of laying on of hands on the sick will be surprised at how exhausting it can be. The priest (or other authorized person) is a minister of God's healing power. That power flows through him or her. Careful preparation is strongly urged on all who minister this power, and time after administration should be spent in intercession and thanksgiving.

Even if there are a large number of people to receive this ministry each must be touched with prayerful care. Normally the officiating minister should stand in front of the person to receive, who may be standing, sitting or kneeling. Both hands are laid firmly and deliberately on the person's head in silence. After a short period the words are said, addressing the person by name, or at least calling them 'my brother' or 'my sister'. Other ministers joining in laying on hands may touch the recipient on the head, shoulders, back and arms. Again the touching should be deliberate and care should be taken not to do anything that might offend the person receiving ministry. It should be remembered that the sick, undergoing many tests and examinations, have frequently experienced physical contact as a violation of their bodily integrity. The hands should be laid on and not moved. Some ministers of healing favour an approach in which the hands do not actually touch but are moved over the person staying a couple of centimetres away from the person. The tradition offers no reason why this should be done and the laying on of hands with actual contact is to be preferred.

See also *Anointing*.

Miscarriage, Abortion, Still-births and Neo-natal Deaths

These form a difficult and related group of experiences and may produce particular difficulties for male ministers and for those with little or no experience of children, childbirth and the like. Professional and experienced counsellors are generally available to those who face them but the minister may well find himself or herself called upon to provide a rite that will bring comfort. No rite written in advance of the particular event can hope to do this, but working with the woman or, if possible, with the woman and her partner, it is possible to celebrate the gift of life, acknowledge loss and grief, handle guilt, and, if necessary, reverently dispose of mortal remains. The rites in this book are concerned with the living and the dying but not directly with the dead. Prayers after death may be useful. One point, however, should be noted: it is contrary to Christian doctrine to baptize the dead. A rite of blessing and naming, with anointing is included here and it is to be hoped that this will meet the immediate needs of many parents and help them express their feelings.

See the relevant section of *Funerals and Ministry to the Bereaved: A Handbook of Funeral Practices and Procedures*, 2nd edition, Church House Publishing, London 1989.

Oils

In most dioceses one of the bishops blesses the oils on Maundy Thursday or on another suitable day. Following traditional practice three oils are normally blessed – the oil for anointing the sick, the oil for anointing before baptism (the oil of catechumens) and chrism, which may be used for post-baptismal anointing, at confirmation, ordination and the consecration of altars and churches.

The oils should be collected annually from the cathedral or wherever the diocesan supply is kept. They should be kept in a safe and seemly place in the church building but not in the same place as the reserved Sacrament. Ecclesiastical supplies can provide various sorts of stocks for keeping them but they may equally be kept in suitable glass containers. Small flasks of the sort used for chemicals, with ground glass stoppers, are particularly suitable. Each container should be clearly labelled with the type of oil that it contains. The pastoral tradition allows the priest to keep some of the oil of the sick at home in case of an emergency call. Again, it should be kept in a safe and seemly place.

It is always better to use oil blessed by the bishop at a diocesan service but a priest may bless oil for anointing the sick. It should be pure olive oil and not a synthetic oil of any sort. The form for blessing is given on page 93.

When the new oils are collected the old oils should be destroyed. Historically, they were poured into the oil lamps and burned, and this may still be done. Otherwise they may be poured away directly to ground, preferably in the churchyard. It is not appropriate for substances set aside for sacramental purposes to be merely disposed of in the rubbish bin or down the drain. Cotton wool used to wipe oil away after anointing should also be burned if at all possible.

Reservation of the Sacrament

Reservation for the communion of the sick is now generally permitted, though the place and method of reservation may be controlled by diocesan regulations. These notes reflect good practice.

1 The sacrament may be reserved in both kinds. The consecrated bread, sufficient for pastoral need, should be kept in a metal container – a pyx or ciborium – and should be renewed frequently, preferably weekly. The older bread should be consumed. Care must be taken to ensure that the consecrated wine is not spilt and it should be kept in a glass bottle with a tight-fitting stopper. Ground glass stoppers are the best sort, not least because they do not absorb any of the wine as a cork might.

2 The sacrament should be reserved in a safe and seemly place. The aumbry, pyx or tabernacle should be locked and the key kept safely. Only the sacrament should be kept there; oils should be stored elsewhere. There should be only one place of reservation in use in any church. The presence of the sacrament may be indicated by a white lamp burning continuously. It should not be an electric light.

See also *Communion of the sick* and *Oils*.

Visiting the Sick

Those who visit the sick do so for a number of reasons, social and pastoral. The minister may well be a regular visitor to a sick person, sometimes bringing communion or administering the laying on of hands and anointing. There is another sort of visitation, found in the Book of

Common Prayer and its revisions, which has fallen out of favour in part because it laid an unfortunate and exclusive stress on sickness as punishment or testing. Yet its main purposes – instruction, exhortation, ministry of the Word, maintenance in faith and intercession – retain their importance and the minister may find occasion to make a more formal visit to sick parishioners. The materials provided here will serve as a resource to be used according to pastoral need.

INDEX OF TOPICS

Anointing 65, 69f, 111
Apostles' Creed 17

Baptism 89–90, 111–13
Behaviour 113
Bereaved, prayers for the 88
Blessing of a home 96–7
Blessing of Oil 62, 93–4
Blessing of persons 94–6
Blessing of Water 91–3

Chaplains 118f
Child, dying 77
Child, death of 84
Child, still-born 84–5
Child, naming of 84
Comfortable words 16
Commendation 80
Communion 41–57, 114f
Confession 18–19, 58–61, 115f
Creed, Apostles' 17

Death, Prayers after 80–5, 86–8
Dying, Rites with 73–81
Dying, Litany for 73–5

Evil, banishing of 96

Faith, Profession of 17–18

Hands, Laying on of 64, 69f, 120
Home, Blessing of 96–7

Lay Ministry 119
Laying on of hands 64, 69f, 120

Miscarriage, etc. 84, 121
Mourning 88

Oil, Blessing of 62, 93–4
Oils 122

Prayers for the Sick 22–40
Preparation, Prayers of 9–13
Profession of Faith 17–18

Reservation of the Sacrament 123

Sentences, biblical 14–15
Soul, commendation of 80
Still-birth 84–5, 121

Visitation of the Sick 14–21, 123f

Water, Blessing of 91–3

INDEX OF PRAYERS BY SUBJECT

Aged 36
Anima Christi 39

Bereaved, comfort of the 88

Child, dying 77
Child, sick 29
Child-birth, before 34–5
Christ, Passion of 32–3
Commendation 80, 82, 87
Crucifix, before 40

Death, sudden 82–3
Death at birth 84–5
Decision-making 35
Doubt 37
Dying 73–81

Evening 38

Faith, Testing of 37
Family and friends 33

General Intercession 22

Healing 25–8
Healing of memories 28
Holy Spirit, invocation of 11, 67
Humble Access 44, 48, 53

Ignatius Loyola 12
Intercession, General 22

Labour, before 34–5
Life-support, withdrawn 79

Medical profession 30
Memories, healing of 28
Ministry, inadequacy of 10
Ministry to the sick 30
Mourners, comfort for 88

Night 39
Nurses 30

Operation, before an 34

Pain, in great 31
Passion of Christ, invocation
    of 32–3
Purity, Collect for 41, 47, 52

Reconciliation between persons
    28
Richard of Chichester 12

Sick and dying 23
Sick person 24
St Patrick's Breastplate 12
Still-birth 84
Sudden death 82–3
Suffering, blessing on 31
Suffering, release from 82
Suffering 24
Suicide 83–4

Thanksgiving after death 81
Thanksgiving for healing 37
Thanksgiving for Holy
    Communion 45–6, 51, 57

Uncertainty 35

INDEX OF PRAYERS BY FIRST LINE

Almighty, everliving God, Maker of mankind 98

Almighty and everliving God, we most heartily 45

Almighty Father, giver of life and health, look 100

Almighty God, Father of mercies 88

Almighty God, Father of our Lord Jesus Christ 18

Almighty God, giver of life and health, hear 30

Almighty God, look on this your servant 73

Almighty God, look with pity 88

Almighty God, our Father in heaven 87

Almighty God, our heavenly Father, we have sinned 20

Almighty God, our heavenly Father, we beseech thee 34

Almighty God, our heavenly Father, what you ask 37

Almighty God, source of human knowledge and skill 30

Almighty God, to whom all hearts are open 52

Almighty God, unto whom all hearts be open 41, 47

Almighty God, you know that we have no power 102

Almighty God, we thank thee for feeding us 51

Almighty God, we thank you for feeding us 57

As you are outwardly anointed 70

As with this holy oil 65

Assist us mercifully, O Lord 100

Be our light in the darkness, O Lord 38

Be present, O merciful God, and protect us 38

Blessed Lord, we ask your loving care 25

Christ be with me, Christ within me 12

Come to her aid, O saints of God 80

Compassionate God, we entrust into your care 83

Deliver your servant N. O Sovereign Lord 76

Depart, O Christian soul 78

Eternal God, whose years extend 36

Father of all, we pray to thee 82

Go forth upon thy journey, Christian soul 78

Go forth upon your journey from this world 78

God be in my head 11

God be your comfort, your strength 95

God of all comfort 58
God of compassion and love 79
God of compassion and mercy 34
God of grace and comfort 27
God of grace, power and mercy 102
God of healing and hope 94
God of love and wisdom 58
God of mercy, source of all healing 70
God of peace, forgive us all 28
God of steadfast love 38
God of the dark night 32
God of the present moment 35
God of the unknown 36
God our Father, your gift of water 93
God our healer, keep us aware of your presence 70
God, our refuge, when human resources fail 37
God the Father lovingly enfold you 97
Grant, O merciful God, we pray 30

Hear us, Almighty and most merciful God 24
Heavenly Father, watch with us over your child 30
Heavenly Father, we thank you that by water 90
Heavenly Father, you anointed your Son Jesus Christ 104
Holy Spirit, come and be with us 11, 67

In the name of God most high 65
Into thy hands, O father and Lord 39
Into your hands, O merciful Saviour 80

Jesus, betrayed, hear my prayer 10
Jesus, King of love, who shared in the life 97
Jesus, you knew a mother's love 85
Jesus you knew pain 33

Keep watch, dear Lord 39

Let the mighty power of the Holy God 96
Let us beseech the Lord, mighty and pitiful 22
Look down, O Lord, from your heavenly throne 38
Lord, by this sweet and saving sign 40
Lord Jesus, I do not find it easy 10
Lord Jesus Christ, Good Shepherd of the sheep 29
Lord Jesus Christ, Son of the living and life-giving 27
Lord Jesus Christ, you knew the agony of dying 84
Lord Jesus Christ, you knew the agony of the garden 83
Lord of all, we thank you for your work in creation 84
Loving God, merciful and forgiving 28
Loving God, our Creator and Redeemer 33

May God the Father bless you 95
Merciful Lord God, constant source of healing 37
Merciful Lord, you sent your Son to be our peace 25

Now may our Lord Jesus Christ himself 95

O almighty Father, who dost heal 26

O almighty God, who hast taught us 94

O Almighty God, whose blessed Son 64

O blessed Jesus, to bring us salvation 34

O God of heavenly powers 29

O God, the creator and sustainer of life 35

O God, the eternal King whom none may overcome 92

O God the strength of the weak 29

O God, who alone canst strengthen 99

O God, who by the prayers of thy holy Apostles 25

O God, who in ordaining the sacrament 91

O God, whose ways are hidden 88

O gracious Father, whose dear Son 31

O gracious Lord Jesus, who didst vouchsafe 23

O holy Lord, almighty Father, everlasting God 26

O Lord, before you brought us into this world 82

O Lord God, look with mercy 36

O Lord God, our heavenly Father, regard we beseech 32

O Lord God, whose mercies are sure 13

O Lord, hear us in our pain and anguish 83

O Lord, hold this sweet and lovely child 85

O Lord, Holy Father, almighty everlasting God 46

O Lord, Holy Father, giver of health 62, 93

O Lord Jesus Christ, conceived by the Holy Spirit 84

O Lord Jesus Christ, God's Word of love 10

O Lord Jesu Christ, Son of the living God 32

O Lord Jesus Christ, the only-begotten Son 77

O Lord Jesus Christ, who by the power of thy word 26

O Lord of all grace and blessing 24

O Lord of the day and of the night 30

O Lord our God, creator of all that exists 35

O Lord our God, send your Holy Spirit to guide us 35

O Lord, your servant N. has come to the end 77

O Lord, who always hears our prayers 28

Our Lord Jesus Christ be with you 94

Remember, O Lord, what thou hast wrought in us 13

Sanctify us all, thou that healest every disease 27

Soul of Christ, sanctify me 39

Sovereign Lord, our God, Almighty, we beseech 26

Teach us, good Lord, to serve thee 12

Thanks be to thee, my Lord Jesus Christ 12

The almighty Lord, who is a most strong tower 66

The almighty Lord who is a strong tower 71

The grace of our Lord Jesus Christ flow 94

129

The Lord bless you and keep you 95

Unto God's gracious mercy and protection 67, 96

Visit this place, O Lord 38

We do not presume to come to this thy table 44, 48

We do not presume to come to this your table 53

We give her back to thee, dear Lord 87

We give thanks to you, Lord our God 81

We rejoice, Lord, that *N.* is well again 29

We thank you, loving Father 82

With painful footsteps, O blessed Lord 31